The Los Angeles Barrio, 1850-1890

A Social History

Richard Griswold del Castillo

UNIVERSITY OF CALIFORNIA PRESS
BERKELEY • LOS ANGELES • LONDON

For Charlie and Ariel

UNIVERSITY OF CALIFORNIA PRESS

BERKELEY AND LOS ANGELES, CALIFORNIA

UNIVERSITY OF CALIFORNIA PRESS, LTD.

LONDON, ENGLAND

FIRST PAPERBACK PRINTING 1982

ISBN 0-520-04773-7

LIBRARY OF CONGRESS CATALOG CARD NUMBER: 78-65460

PRINTED IN THE UNITED STATES OF AMERICA

The paper used in this publication meets the minimum requirements
of ANSI/NISO Z39.48-1992 (R 1997) (*Permanence of Paper*). ∞

CONTENTS

List of Tables, Maps, and Illustrations   vii
Preface   xi

1. EL PUEBLO DE LOS ANGELES   1
   The Indian Tradition   1
   The Settlement of Los Angeles   4
   Early Population Data   7
   The California Culture   10
   The Age of the Ranchos   13
   Californio Politics   19
   American Contacts   21
   The Mexican War in Los Angeles   25

2. EXCLUSION FROM A DEVELOPING ECONOMY   30
   Socioeconomic Changes   41
   Occupational Mobility   51

3. CHANGES IN THE URBAN FAMILY   62
   The Traditional Family   63
   Relations Between the Sexes   69
   Marriage and Intermarriage   74
   The Family and Fertility   77
   The Family and Education   84
   The Family and Literacy   90
   The Family and Socioeconomic Mobility   92

4. AN EMERGING ETHNIC CONSCIOUSNESS   103
   Violence   105
   Discrimination   115
   Repatriation   119
   Ethnic Newspapers and Organizations   124

5. ISOLATION: GEOGRAPHIC, POLITICAL, SPIRITUAL   139
     Geographic Segregation   141
     Political Decline   150
     Religious Segregation   161

CONCLUSION   171

APPENDIX A. THE CENSUSES   177
     1. Census Sources Used in Tables   177
     2. Discussion of Methods and Procedures   177
     3. Statistical Errors in the Census   178
     4. The 1850 and 1852 California Censuses   179
     5. Problems in Classifying
         Mexican-Americans in the Census   180
     6. Analysis of Mexican-American Family
         Relationships   182

APPENDIX B. MEXICAN-AMERICAN OCCUPATIONS,
            1850–1880   185

APPENDIX C. THE LOS ANGELES CITY DIRECTORIES
            AND SOCIAL RESEARCH   188

Glossary   191
Bibliography   193
Index   213

TABLES, MAPS, AND
ILLUSTRATIONS

Tables

1. Spanish and Mexican Populations of Los Angeles District, 1781–1844   8
2. Los Angeles District's Growth, Based on the 1836 and 1844 Censuses   9
3. Population Growth and Stabilization in Los Angeles, 1850–1880   35
4. Migratory Population Changes, 1844–1880   36
5. Comparative Persistence Rates for Los Angeles Mexican-Americans and Selected Urban Communities   37
6. The Mexican-Born Population of Los Angeles, 1844–1880   40
7. Mexican-American Property-Holders in Los Angeles, 1850–1870   47
8. Persisting Property-Holders in Selected Periods   48
9. Social Characteristics of Persisting Property-Owners   50
10. Occupational Structure Among Los Angeles Mexican-Americans, 1844–1880   53
11. Mexican-Americans Employed in Traditional Skilled Occupations, 1844–1880   58
12. Mexican-Americans Employed in New Occupations, 1850–1880   59
13. Spanish-Speaking Heads of Households, 1844–1880   66
14. Death Rate Among a Sample of 250 Mexican-Americans in Los Angeles, 1877–1887   67
15. Mexican-American Women Working Outside the Home, 1850–1880   74
16. Intermarriage, 1856–1875   76

17. Age Distribution of Married Mexican-American
    Women   78
18. Birthrate for City and County
    Mexican-Americans, 1850–1870   80
19. School Attendance of Los Angeles Children,
    1860–1880   86
20. Literacy Related to Place of Birth   91
21. Literacy of Heads of Household by Type of
    Family   93
22. Literacy of Heads of Household by Occupational
    Status   94
23. Literacy of Heads of Household by Categories of
    Wealth   95
24. Family Types, 1844–1880   99
25. Distribution of Income by Type of Family,
    1850–1870   100
26. Persisting Socioeconomic Mobility by Type of
    Family, 1844–1880   101
27. Mexican-American Participation on Juries,
    1863–1873   118
28. Spanish-Language Newspapers in Los Angeles,
    1850–1900   126
29. Organizations in Los Angeles, 1850–1900   136
30. Mexican-American Property-Owners and Value
    of Holdings by Section of City, 1861–1876   144
31. Spanish-Surnamed Population by Wards, 1880   145
32. Los Angeles Californio Members of Local and
    State Democratic Committees and
    Conventions, 1850–1860   155
33. Californios from Los Angeles Elected or
    Appointed to State or Local Offices, 1850–1859   156
34. Los Angeles Mexican-American Office-Holders
    by Level of Office, 1850–1879   159
35. Social Characteristics of Los Angeles
    Mexican-American Political Leaders,
    1850–1880   162
36. Social Statistics for Los Angeles Chicanos, 1880
    and 1970   175

Maps

1. Los Angeles in 1849   142
2. Chicano Property-Holders, 1861–1876   143
3. Chicano Residence Patterns, 1872–1887   147

Illustrations

1. The last Mexican governor, Pío Pico.   15
2. The Pueblo of Los Angeles in 1850.   16
3. A panorama of Sonora Town in 1870.   43
4. Adobe brick-making.   44
5. A Mexicano family with Gabrielino relatives.   55
6. A merchant and his family in front of their store.   56
7. Baptisms in Los Angeles 1844–1873.   81
8. Young Mexicanos on an early baseball team.   82
9. A young teamster hauling wood for the city.   111
10. Calle de los Negros or "Nigger Alley," as it
    appeared in 1882.   112
11. Mexicano caballeros parading down Main Street.   129
12. Panoramic view of Sonora Town in 1879.   130
13. Antonio Coronel, one of the few Mexicanos
    elected as mayor of Los Angeles after 1850.   165
14. The pueblo church, Nuestra Señora la Reina de
    Los Angeles.   166

PREFACE

Between 1848 and 1900, a generous lifetime for men of the nineteenth century, the Spanish-speaking peoples of the southwestern United States changed from a Mexican frontier society into an ethnic group marginal to both Mexican and Anglo-American cultures. The main theme of this work is the economic, familial, societal, and geopolitical metamorphosis of this unique Spanish-language culture. How did the new ethnic group evolve?

In attempting to answer this question, writers and scholars have suggested that racial discrimination, cultural oppression, and outright violence have been major forces molding the Mexican-American experience. While partially concurring in this view, I would add that since the late nineteenth century, Mexican-American history has also been characterized by creative and constructive responses to changing circumstances.

After the Mexican-American War of 1848, the most rapid modifications in the frontier Mexican way of life occurred in the towns. Here, thousands of displaced Mexicans met the most brutal as well as the most progressive aspects of the new Anglo-American order. Rural Mexican culture in the Southwest changed slowly in the decades after 1848. In Arizona and New Mexico, rural life continued as it had before the war. Anglo encroachments took decades to diminish the numbers who lived on the land. The ranchos and farms of Southern California, where the majority of California Mexicans lived, were for some time isolated from the thousands of gold-seekers who inundated the North.

In 1850, Los Angeles, California, was the largest Mexican town in the United States. By 1880 it had become an American city, and the Spanish-speaking residents of the original pueblo found themselves living in a barrio called Sonora Town. Thus I have chosen to study the dynamics of change in the pueblo of Los Angeles.

No one has yet studied the history of how the ethnic community of Sonora Town came into existence, or the changing nature of its social composition and culture. Leonard Pitt and a few others have discussed the Mexicans of Los Angeles as part of larger studies, but most histories of early Los Angeles give little attention to the Mexican-Americans living there. I hope that the present study will enlighten those who seek the historical origins of the urban Chicano, be of value to those who are concerned with the effects of modernization on traditional societies, and help to inform those who are attempting to improve contemporary social conditions.

Leonard Pitt's *The Decline of the Californios* was the original inspiration for this project. His well-documented and original interpretations of the economic and social decline of the *hacendados* prompted me to attempt this social history of the thousands of laborers and semi-skilled workers who constituted the mass of the Spanish-speaking population.

The methodology of the New Urban History, particularly the quantitatively based work of Stephan Thernstrom and Richard Sennett, shaped this study. It was from them that I first learned of the possibility of "doing history from the bottom up." Almost all of the quantitative studies published to date have been concerned with communities east of the Mississippi. Perhaps this book will be followed by others that focus on the minorities of the American Southwest. The anthropologist Octavio Romano-V. has urged historians and social scientists to look at "traditional" Chicano culture from a more dynamic point of view. I share his concern that Mexican-Americans should be regarded as actively participating in the shaping of their history and culture.

I am grateful to the many people and institutions who contributed their time and effort in the shaping of this book. Richard Weiss, Associate Professor of History at the University of California, Los Angeles, was instrumental in encouraging me to begin my research when I was a doctoral candidate there. He, along with Professors Gary Nash and Melvin Pollner, offered valuable suggestions at various points in the first-draft stage. Professors James Wilkie and Oscar Martínez reviewed the completed manuscript and proposed thematic and structural changes. Welcome criticism and encouragement came from Professor Leonard Pitt, who took time from a busy schedule to read the entire work. Professor David Weber, my former colleague at San Diego State University, gave a close scrutiny to Chapter 1, thereby improving its historical accuracy. Of course, even after all the correction and criticism, errors are bound to remain, and they are my full responsibility.

I am indebted to Bill Mason and the staff of the Los Angeles Museum of Natural History for their countless hours of help. The staff of the Huntington Library was also very helpful in locating and researching nineteenth-century documents. Los Angeles City College District, the UCLA Computer Network, and the Computer Center at San Diego State University all provided many hours of consultation and computer time.

Financial assistance from the Ford Foundation and UCLA's Patent Fund, together with the generous services provided by San Diego State University, made typing expenses easier to bear. My editor, Milton Savage, whom I count as a good friend after months of unrelenting work, deserves much of the credit for making the final version more readable. I am also indebted to Marjorie Hughes, of the University of California Press, for her help in preparing the final draft. Finally, to my wife, Maryann, I owe special thanks for her steadfast support throughout the turmoil.

CHAPTER ONE

El Pueblo de Los Angeles

When Commodore Robert F. Stockton stood atop Fort Hill in 1846, looking down on the Mexican pueblo of Nuestra Señora la Reina de Los Angeles de Porciúncula, what he saw was the result of the blending of three cultural traditions—Indian, Spanish, and Mestizo. It bore almost no resemblance to modern metropolitan Los Angeles.

Below him he could make out the plaza, a barren open space surrounded by a cluster of adobes almost indistinguishable from the brown grass that shimmered in the summer heat. To the east, between the pueblo and the stands of willows that marked the river channel—a distance of about half a mile—hundreds of cattle grazed slowly near dry irrigation ditches that led to a few irregularly shaped fields of beans, corn, squash, and peppers. In the heat of the day, the few vaqueros and farmers in the shallow valley stood motionless, as though time had stopped. But this seemingly changeless scene, reflecting as it did the earth out of which it had been made, had not always appeared so.

The Indian Tradition

The first families migrated into the area now known as Southern California at least 20,000 years ago. Anthropologists, who group California Indians linguistically, believe that these first settlers spoke Shoshonean, a language related to the Comanche, Aztec, and Pueblo Indian languages. Evidence indicates that these Shoshonean-speaking peoples probably migrated through the Owens Valley from somewhere in the southwestern United States or northern Mexico.[1]

Culturally, all of the Indians of the Los Angeles basin shared the same life-style. By 1770 they numbered about 5,000 and were divided into many tribes. They spoke various dialects of Shoshone, but are all referred to as "Gabrielino" after the mission the Spanish established on their lands. They lived in an area bordered by the Santa Susana Mountains to the north, the Mojave Desert to the east, Aliso Creek to the south, and San Clemente Island to the west.[2]

Many elements of their culture facilitated the eventual assimilation of the Gabrielinos into the Spanish mission and hacienda systems. Intermarriage between the Gabrielinos and the Spanish, Mestizo, and Black settlers further aided assimilation. As was the case throughout the Southwest, the Hispano settlers in turn adopted certain elements of the native Indian culture. Thus, during the eighty-odd years of Hispanic contact, a subtle fusion of Spanish, Mexican-Indian, Black, and native Indian cultures took place on biological, ideological, and material levels.[3]

On the ideological level, for example, similarities be-

1. The major historical and anthropological studies of the Indians of Los Angeles are: Alfred L. Kroeber, *Handbook of the Indians of California;* John W. Caughey (ed.), *The Indians of Southern California in 1852;* Alfred Robinson, *Life in California: A Historical Account of the Origin, Customs and Traditions of the Indians of Alta California;* William Wilcox Robinson, *The Indians of Los Angeles: The Story of the Liquidation of a People;* Hugo Reid, *The Indians of Los Angeles County* (a reprint of articles appearing in the *Los Angeles Star,* Feb. 21–Aug. 1, 1952; in Los Angeles County Museum of Natural History; Bernice E. Johnston, *California's Gabrielino Indians.*

2. Robert F. Heizer (ed.), *The Indians of Los Angeles County: Hugo Reid's Letters of 1852,* Introduction; Alfred L. Kroeber, "The Native Population of California," in Robert F. Heizer and Mary Ann Whipple (eds.), *The California Indians: A Source Book,* p. 71.

3. For another study of the cultural fusion of Hispanic and Indio peoples, see Frances Leon Swadish, *Los Primeros Pobladores: Hispanic Americans of the Ute Frontier,* ch. 2.

tween Indian and Spanish religious practices facilitated cultural mixing. Like the Franciscans, the Gabrielinos believed in a hierarchy of spiritual authority. They worshiped a creator god named "Chingichnich" or "Chungichnish," a virgin god named "Chukit," and a pantheon of lesser deities. The Gabrielinos had developed a complex ritual involving the use of jimsonweed mixed with salt water which, when taken as a food, represented a spiritual purification similar to the Eucharist. The Gabrielinos also had religious initiation rites and mystical chants and songs.[4]

There were other similarities. The social customs of the Gabrielinos closely paralleled those of the Spanish settlers: elaborate wedding ceremonies, a paternalistic authoritarian family, and strong kinship ties were common to both cultures. Politically, the Indian rancherías resembled the cacique system in Mexico. Local chiefs exercised despotic authority over small villages comprised of kinship groupings. How much the Californio culture in the Mexican era was influenced by Indian antecedents is a matter of conjecture. We know that the early settlers did adopt some local games, the use of woven baskets, and the use of symbolic money. The willow cooking shelters that adjoined the adobe houses of the rancho period were clearly adaptations of the Indian jacals.[5]

In matters of medicine, the Indian influence was probably more pervasive. The Indians taught the Spaniards to treat arrow wounds and to use such healing herbs as anise and wild hemp. The absence of doctors in the frontier pueblo accustomed the pobladores to rely on an occasional Indian shaman. It is not known exactly how much of this California Indian folk medicine found its way into the health practices of the early settlers, but the local curanderos, as in Mexico, probably borrowed elements of the native healing arts. In general, the Spanish and Mexican pobladores assimi-

4. Kroeber, Handbook, pp. 620–627.
5. Ana Begue Packman, Leather Dollars: Short Stories of the Pueblo of Los Angeles, pp. 36–37.

lated and modified elements of an Indian way of life
that was well adapted to the unique environment of
Southern California.[6]

Until the arrival of the first settlers, the Gabrielinos
prospered in relative peace despite the density of their
settlements. At least 40, perhaps as many as 70, Indian
rancherías—each averaging about 130 families—had to
share a limited food supply.[7] They had developed a del-
icate ecological balance among themselves and with
the land. Because of this, together with the density and
peacefulness of the Gabrielino population, the entry of
the Spanish into Southern California was the beginning
of a disaster.

The Settlement of Los Angeles

Spain delayed settling Alta California for over 200
years, largely because of difficulties encountered in establishing frontier outposts in Sonora (Mexico), New
Mexico, and Baja California. New expeditions were
costly, and for centuries the Spanish Crown had regarded their New World possessions as sources of rev-
enue, not as areas for large-scale investment.

This neglect ended in 1769 when Visitador José Galvez organized a series of expeditions to explore Alta
California. One of these first expeditions named the
Los Angeles River. On August 2, 1769, Captain Gaspar
de Portolá, along with Fray Junípero Serra and a contingent of soldiers and Indians, camped near the river,
naming it El Río de Nuestra Señora la Reina de Los
Angeles de Porciúncula. Here they encountered an In-

6. In 1838, Mariano G. Vallejo published *La botanica general de los
remedios experimentados,* a compendium of local medicinal cures,
many of them obviously borrowed from the Indians. Hubert Howe
Bancroft, *California Pastoral, 1789–1848,* pp. 625–627; Richard
Griswold del Castillo, "Health and the Mexican-Americans in Los
Angeles, 1850–1887," *J. Mex.-Am. Hist.*

7. John W. Caughey, *California,* p. 20; "Nombre primeros de
algunos de los lugares del Los Angeles County . . ." (ms., Coronel
Collection, L.A. County Mus. Nat. Hist.); Kroeber, *Handbook,*
map: "Native Sites in Part of Southern California."

dian ranchería of the Yang-na people, and noted that the location seemed suitable for a pueblo. Twelve years later the new governor, Felipe de Neve, sent out an expedition to establish pueblos, missions, and presidios, in order to secure Spain's claim to this remote frontier region. On about September 4, 1781 (historians are not sure of the exact date), a contingent of 44 settlers and 4 soldiers founded the community.[8]

There were 11 families in this first contingent, later described as persons "whose blood was a mixture of Indian and Negro with traces of a few Spanish. . . ."[9] A more exact description of the early ethnic composition of these pioneers counts 8 Mulattos, 9 Indians, 2 Negroes, 1 Mestizo, and 1 person listed as "Chino."[10] References to these people and later colonists as Spanish, therefore, are based on their political status as subjects, not on their ethnic identity.

As they had done in New Mexico, Arizona, and Texas, the Spanish in California chose sites for their pueblos, presidios, and missions near established Indian villages. Not only did the preexistence of an Indian settlement indicate that water, fertile land, and game were nearby, but it also promised a ready source of labor and—as was usually the case—women. These early pobladores chose a site near the Yang-na ranchería located on the west bank of the Río Porciúncula.

Under the terms of the Spanish laws governing colonization (de Neve's *Reglamento* of June 1, 1779), only adult males were eligible for land grants. Those who qualified received a town lot (solare) and 4 fields (suertes or bejesas) of 200 varas each (167 meters), along with loans of foodstuffs and farming imple-

8. Some controversy surrounds the original name of Los Angeles. Most authors have used the name Nuestra Señora la Reina de Los Angeles, but Father Francis Weber maintains that the original appellation omitted la Reina altogether. See Rev. Francis J. Weber, *El Pueblo de Los Angeles: An Enquiry in Early Appellations.*

9. Bancroft, *Pastoral*, p. 251.

10. Carey McWilliams, *North from Mexico: The Spanish-Speaking People of the United States*, p. 36.

ments. But after five years, due to expulsions and defections, only 8 of the original 11 men remained to receive title to their lands in September 1786. Of those who remained, most were peasant farmers recruited from northern Mexico, men already accustomed to making a hard living in the desert.[11]

By 1791 the new pueblo had become one of the most prosperous settlements in California. Only nearby Mission San Gabriel surpassed it in crop and livestock production. But due to the remoteness of the colony, the forbidding desert barrier, and the lack of gold or silver, there was little incentive for additional settlers to make the long, dangerous journey north to Alta California. In 1800, after almost twenty years of colonization, Los Angeles had a population of only 139, including 28 families. There was now a town hall, a granary, a chapel, an army barracks, and 29 dwellings.[12]

The Spanish authorities' problems in recruiting settlers for the colony had brought about a change in policy. After 1791 the governors began sending numbers of convicts and orphans. This forced immigration, which lasted throughout the Spanish period and was continued by the Mexican government until 1846, antagonized the native Californios, who were more concerned with moral purity than with population growth. The government sent convict and orphan expeditions in 1825, 1829, and 1830, accounting for most of the Mexican immigration in those years.[13]

Mexico made some attempts to attract skilled artisans and farmers in addition to the convicts. One example was the colonization effort of 1833–34, organized by Gomez Fárias in Mexico and led by José María Padrés and José María Híjar. This scheme

11. Thomas Workman Temple II, "Soldiers and Settlers of the Expedition of 1781," *Q. Hist. Soc. So. Calif.*, p. 100; Bancroft, *Pastoral*, p. 249.

12. William Wilcox Robinson, *Los Angeles from the Days of the Pueblo*, p. 20; and Bancroft, *Pastoral*, p. 258.

13. Leonard Pitt, *The Decline of the Californios: A Social History of the Spanish-Speaking Californians, 1846–1890*, p. 6.

attempted to entice artisans to California with promises of expropriated mission lands. The new settlers eventually established themselves in the Sonoma Valley, but the suspicions of local political authorities led to their disbandment. Remnants of the colony found their way to Los Angeles and some, like Don Ygnacio Coronel and Felipe Alanis, later became wealthy and influential men in the community.[14]

Early Population Data

A rough sketch of the sources of Los Angeles' growth before the Mexican war can be made from the censuses taken by the Spanish and Mexican governments (see Table 1). Population data for 1781 is based on the mission records and on Bancroft's copies of the Spanish archives; the originals of these documents have been destroyed.

The Mexican official censuses taken in 1830, 1836 and 1844 are much more detailed and complete.[15] From these two documents several trends emerge (see Table 2). First, the native-born population of Los Angeles nearly doubled in less than ten years, indicating a high birthrate and prosperous economic conditions. Second, immigration from other regions of California and the Southwest declined after 1836. Because of the generous land-grant policy of the Mexican government, many of those moving into the area settled on outlying ranchos rather than in the pueblo itself. Third, migration from northern Mexico was a major source of population; most Angelenos who had been born in Mexico came from Sonora or Baja California.

In reviewing the Mexican and Anglo-American cen-

14. C. Alan Hutchinson's *Frontier Settlement in Mexican California: The Padrés–Híjar Colony* has a detailed history of this expedition. See also Angustias de la Guerra Ord, *Occurrences in Hispanic California;* and Hubert Howe Bancroft, *The History of California,* 1825–1840, vol. 3, pp. 259–280.

15. J. Gregg Layne (comp.), "The First Census of the Los Angeles District," *Q. Hist. Soc. So. Calif.;* Marie E. Northrup (comp.), "The Los Angeles Padrón of 1844, *ibid.*

TABLE 1

Spanish and Mexican Populations of
Los Angeles District, 1781–1844

	1781[a]	1830[b]	1836[c]	1844[d]
Men	11	258	553	627
Women	15	264	421	500
Children (under 18)	15	242	651	720
Domesticated Indians	nl	198	533	650
Foreigners	nl	nl	50	53
Total	41	962	2,208	2,550

nl = not listed in original census

Note: The Los Angeles District included many not living in the pueblo of Los Angeles.

a. Thomas Workman Temple II, "Soldiers and Settlers of the Expedition of 1781," *Q. Hist. Soc. So. Calif.* 15 (1931–1933): 99–104. Three others arrived after 1781, bringing the total to 44.

b. William N. Charles, "The Transcription and Translation of the Old Mexican Documents of the Los Angeles County Archives," *Q. Hist. Soc. So. Calif.* 20, no. 2 (June 1938): 84–88.

c. J. Gregg Layne (comp.), "The First Census of the Los Angeles District," *Q. Hist. Soc. So. Calif.* 18 (September–December 1936): 81–114.

d. Marie E. Northrup (comp.), "The Los Angeles Padrón of 1844," *Q. Hist. Soc. So. Calif.* 42 (1960): 360–422.

suses for the period 1830–1880, an unexpected finding is that the ratio of the sexes (number of males per 100 females) rose dramatically (see Table 1). The years 1836 and 1844 mark high points, after which the ratio declined. These high points coincided with political upheavals: the Alvarado rebellion of 1836 and the Micheltorena revolt of 1845 attracted hundreds of

TABLE 2

Los Angeles District's Growth,
Based on the 1836 and 1844 Censuses

Place of birth	1836[a]		1844[b]	
	Number	Percentage	Number	Percentage
Los Angeles City	1,038	47	2,018	79
California and the Southwest	939	43	325	13
Northern Mexico	140	6	110	4
Southern Mexico	41	2	44	2
Foreign	50	2	53	2
Totals	2,208	100	2,550	100

a. J. Gregg Layne (comp.), "The First Census of the Los Angeles District," *Q. Hist. Soc. So. Calif.* 18 (September–December 1936): 81–114.

b. Marie E. Northrup (comp.), "The Los Angeles Padrón of 1844," *Q. Hist. Soc. So. Calif.* 42 (1960): 360–422.

citizen-soldiers to the district. Thus these excesses of men to women were probably a result of military maneuvering during temporary political emergencies.[16]

16. David J. Weber, "Mexico's Far Northern Frontier, 1821–1854: Historiography Askew," *Western Hist. Q.* The sex ratio for the Mexican-American population, 1830–1880, was as follows: in 1830, there were 97 males to 100 females; 1836, *131;* 1844, *125;* 1850, *106;* 1860, *118;* 1870, *99;* 1880, *78.* This ratio is for adults only, defined as those over 20 years of age. An analysis of the age/sex distributions for the years 1844–1880 reveals that the bulk of the sex imbalance in 1844 and 1860 was in groups over 20 years of age, indicating that sex differences in birth and infant mortality probably were not a factor. The extremely low sex ratio for 1880 may point to a higher death rate for male infants in earlier years— but this is not an unequivocal finding, because of the high degree of geographic mobility in the population.

The California Culture

Frontier Los Angeles was far removed from the main currents of change in the Mexican Republic. This isolation reinforced the development of a unique way of life. Social and political contacts with central Mexico were infrequent, because a vast desert filled with hostile Indians separated the two regions. As a result, the cultural waters of central Mexico and of the frontier flowed in different channels. Ygnacio Sepúlveda noted as much: The Californios, having "settled in a remote part from the center of government, isolated from and almost unaided by the rest of the Mexican states and with very rare chances of communication with the rest of the world, they, in time, formed a society whose habits, customs, and manners differed in many essential particulars from the other people of Mexico. . . ."[17] Specifically, he believed that the Californios developed a less "restless spirit" and a "milder form of independence" than their cousins to the south. They were more egalitarian in social manners but, paradoxically, were more concerned with the purity of their Spanish blood.

It was true that the Californios were little influenced by the Inquisition and the military despotism, latifundian peonage, and centralized control that characterized the history of regions of central Mexico and portions of Texas and New Mexico. The Californios also lacked the experience of intense Indian warfare, with its constant threat of extermination, that hung over Hispanic Arizona and New Mexico. The custom of rewarding presidio soldiers with land grants made for a remarkable degree of upward mobility and created the fortunes of many leading families.[18]

The egalitarianism of Californio society decreased later when the province became wealthier and more populous. José María Amador, an old soldier who lived

17. Bancroft, *Pastoral,* p. 282.
18. Leon G. Campbell, "The First Californios: Presidial Society in Spanish California, 1769–1822," *J. of the West.*

through the change to a more stratified social order, remembered that "In my first years there were very few social distinctions—the officials and their families, the sergeants, corporals, soldiers, and their relatives exchanged horses during social gatherings and expected only that all were honorable men. Later, following the development of the country, which increased wealth and population, separate classes were formed. . . ."[19]

Of course, Amador was not considering the California Indians as part of the social system. They were the most notable exception to this view of an egalitarian society. The Spaniards and Mexicans alike considered the Indians to be their social inferiors. Outnumbering the Spanish-stock settlers, they lived as virtual slaves on the large ranchos after the secularization of the mission lands in 1834. Even a sympathetic observer such as Padre Durán remarked, "The Indian evinces no other ambition than to possess a little more savage license, even though it involves a thousand oppressions of servitude. . . ."[20] Amador's view of a classless society in the early years must certainly be tempered by an awareness of the social status of Indians.

The native-born Californio ranked the Mexican immigrants and soldiers with the Indians in the lowest orders. For the Californio upper class, the Mexican-born were "cholos," little more than thieves and public nuisances. This was particularly true of the *cholo* troops that Governor Micheltorena brought with him from Mexico in 1844. Described as "thieves and pickpockets scoured from the jails," the soldiers only heightened the class prejudices of the Californio against the

19. José María Amador, "Memorias sobre la historia de California" (ms., Bancroft Library), p. 266. The original Spanish reads: "En mis primeros años había muy poca distinción social—los oficiales y sus familias, los sargentos, cabos y soldaderos y los surgos alternaban pintos en reuniones solo se exigía que fuese gente honrada. Leugo generalmente según fueron desarrollandose los recoursos aumentando la riqueza y creciendo la población con gentes de fuera se fueron separando las clases. . . . "
20. C. Alan Hutchinson, *Frontier Settlement*, p. 233.

Indian-stock Mestizo.[21] The "gente de razón" regarded themselves as pure-blooded sons and daughters of the conquistadores, racially and culturally superior to the lowly Indian and Mexican.

The Franciscan mission system also helped to shape Californio culture. The California missions were different from the institutions that developed in other areas of the Southwest; they were on a larger scale and much more prosperous than those of Arizona, New Mexico, or Texas. The New Mexico missions were small churches located near Pueblo Indian villages. Unlike those in Alta California, they owned no lands and pursued no program of concentrating diverse tribes into a central location.[22]

Indian labor formed the backbone of the California mission system, although only about one-twentieth of the native peoples were missionized by 1836. The Franciscans introduced hundreds of new plants and animals such as wheat, barley, and alfalfa, and cattle, horses, pigs, and sheep; and they trained the Indians to cultivate them. The Indians became *vaqueros,* farmers, and craftsmen. This pool of trained labor made possible the growth of the rancho and, later, the agricultural economy of California.[23]

The Indians in turn taught the missionaries, soldiers, and settlers their foods, medicines, games, and languages. But the natives were the losers in this historical exchange. Besides transmitting Western "civilization," the newcomers also contributed measles, typhoid, influenza, smallpox, and cholera.

As these diseases reduced the native Indian popula-

21. Ord, *Occurrences,* p. 52. Bancroft has listed those Californio writers who expressed their opinions of the *cholos* in *History of California,* 1841–1845, vol. 4, p. 365.

22. For a comparison of the New Mexico and California missions, see Hubert Howe Bancroft, *The History of Arizona and New Mexico, 1530–1888,* pp. 160–162 and 279, and his *History of California,* 1801–1824, vol. 2, pp. 107, 112, 160, and 552.

23. Gabriel Marcella, "Spanish-Mexican Contributions to the Southwest," *J. Mex.-Am. Hist.*

tion, contacts with the pobladores and soldiers resulted in genetic assimilation. Throughout the Spanish and Mexican periods, intermarriage and illicit unions between the Gabrielinos and the settlers were common, producing many *hijos de país* of Indian lineage.[24] Mexican families customarily adopted orphaned or abandoned Indian children and considered them as their own; in some families these Indian children were employed as live-in servants and laborers.[25] By 1850, through the processes of missionization, secularization, intermarriage, adoption, and employment, remnants of the local Indian way of life had become a living part of the Hispanic culture of Los Angeles.

The Age of the Ranchos

During the Mexican period and well into the American, ranchos were an important part of pueblo society. In 1844 there were no industries in Los Angeles except those dependent upon the rancho economy. A listing of pueblo occupations from the census of that year reveals this interdependence: saddlers, farm workers, blacksmiths, tavernkeepers, ranchers, laborers, and servants made up the bulk of the occupations of those employed in the city. The rancho formed the social as well as the economic heart of the pueblo well into the 'sixties.

Authors have eulogized the lives of the hacendados, giving Anglo-Americans visions of an idyllic and romantic society. Writing in the 1880's, Hubert Howe Bancroft conjectured that before the Americans came, ". . . supremest happiness was theirs; the happiness that

24. The earliest record of a legal union between a settler and a Gabrielino occurred in 1784, when José Carlos Rosas and his brother married Indian women at the San Gabriel Mission. W. W. Robinson, *Indians of Los Angeles*, p. 13; Caughey, *California*, p. 23.

25. "Madrinas . . . have a great taste for keeping Indian children til they become of age or marry; there are many orphans whom their parents have left to the possession and care of particular friends, and others for whom the probate courts have appointed guardians. . . ." B. D. Wilson quoted in Caughey, *Indians of So. Calif.*, p. 51.

knows no want, that harbors no unobtainable longing,
no desires that might not be gratified, the happiness of
ignorance, of absence of pain. . . ."[26] Summarizing the
quality of life on the southern ranchos, this statement
and others like it applied only to the wealthy class. The
vast· majority of Mexican Indians, Mestizos, and other
mixtures achieved what happiness they could through
hard work. They were underlings, subservient to the
patrón and to a life-style organized for the benefit of an
elite.

As the rancheros became more dominant in the social and economic life of Mexican California, the
egalitarianism of the early years gave way to a more
hierarchical society. Every aspect of rancho life was
controlled by a rigid, highly organized work routine.
Besides the Indian vaqueros and servants, there were
different levels of overseers: *mayordomos de los chaponeras*
were in charge of the servants, and there were other
overseers of varying degrees of authority.[27]

The role of women in rancho society was rigidly defined by tradition and work routine. For most, life was
marked by unremitting drudgery, a notable exception
to the pastoral myth. José Carmen del Lugo, who lived
on a rancho during the Mexican regime, recalled something of the women's role: "At three o'clock in the
morning the entire family was summoned to their
prayers. After this, the women betook themselves to
the kitchen and other domestic chores such as sweeping, cleaning, and dusting, and so on. . . . Woman's
labor lasted till seven or eight in the morning. After
this they were busy cooking, sewing, or washing."[28]

26. Bancroft, *Pastoral*, p. 264. This pastoral idealization was
reflected by later Anglo historians who emphasized the Spanish
over the Mestizo culture in California. Carey McWilliams has called
this a "fantasy heritage." For a detailed discussion of the historiography of this pastoral myth, see Pitt, *Decline*, ch. 16, and McWilliams, *North from Mexico*, ch. 2.
27. Horace Bell, *Reminiscences of a Ranger, or Early Times in
Southern California*, p. 227; Jo Mora, *Californios*.
28. José Carmen del Lugo, "Vida de un Ranchero," *Q. Hist.
Soc. So. Calif.*, p. 21.

1. The last Mexican governor, Pío Pico, with his nieces and daughter. Left to right: Marianita Alvarado, Leonora Pico, Pío Pico, Trinidad Ortega. Courtesy of San Diego Title and Trust Company, San Diego.

2. The Pueblo of Los Angeles as it appeared in 1850. Taken from a model. Courtesy of Title Insurance and Trust Company, Los Angeles.

Certainly an easy life was obtainable for a few, but only by the labor of many.

Fiestas there were to be sure, but even these seemed to be related to work. Perhaps the largest and longest fiestas were the rodeos held in January and April, when the alcalde decreed a public holiday so that the whole pueblo might assist in the roundup. This was an occasion for a good deal of social leveling, since all able-bodied men and women worked at the many tasks at hand.

During the rodeo the pobladores sorted the herds that had become mixed on the open range, branded the new calves, castrated the bulls, and killed and skinned hundreds of cattle. The work lasted three or four days. After sundown the assembled vaqueros, gente de razón, and common folk held a fiesta—with drinking, singing, and dancing—sometimes all night. Horace Bell tells of attending one exhausting rodeo in San Diego with over 2,000 people present. It lasted, nonstop, two days and nights.[29]

The wealthiest rancheros, besides owning vast areas of land around the pueblo of Los Angeles, also owned town houses. Their two-story adobes surrounded the dusty plaza. Don Ygnacio del Valle, part owner of Rancho San Francisco, with over 48,000 acres, lived on the east side of the plaza. Close by were Don Vicente Sanchez, owner of Rancho Paseo de la Tijera (Las Cienegas) with over 4,000 acres, and Don Francisco Sepúlveda, who owned Rancho Vicente y Santa Monica with more than 30,000 acres.[30]

Well into the 1860's, the plaza was the residence of the wealthy and, as such, it remained the political and social center of the Hispanic community. It was also the place where the community celebrated its traditional secular and religious fiestas, events which had a

29. Mora, *Californios,* pp. 82–103; Bell, *Reminiscences,* pp. 126–127.
30. Leonard Pitt, "Submergence of the Mexican in California, 1846–1890: A History of Culture Conflict and Acculturation" (Ph.D. diss.), p. 292; W. W. Robinson, *Los Angeles from the Days of the Pueblo,* pp. 32–36.

collective significance unifying the town and reaffirm-
ing traditional loyalties.

Among the most important of the religious celebrations was the Fiesta de Corpus Cristi, coming forty
days after Easter. This occasion served as a reminder to
the pobladores that the bases of authority were religious as well as economic. During the fiesta, each plaza
family constructed an elaborate and expensive altar in
front of their house. Then, in religious procession, the
common folk paid homage at each altar. In the early
'fifties, Harris Newmark observed the festivities: "The
procession would start from the church after the four
o'clock service and proceed around the plaza from altar
to altar. There boys and girls, carrying banners and
flowers and robed or dressed in white, paused for a
formal worship. . . ."[31]

Another fiesta day that maintained the solidarity between the upper and lower classes, and symbolically
unified the outlying ranchos with the pueblo, was the
celebration of Los Pastores. This fiesta lasted from December 25th to January 6th, during which time a procession led by 12 townspeople, dressed to represent bib-
lical and secular characters, slowly made its way from
the outlying ranchos. They usually began at Rancho
Los Feliz and ended at the plaza. It took about a week
for the procession to reach the pueblo, since they
stopped at most of the houses along the way for food,
drink, and song.[32] Once at the plaza, the procession
paid homage to the respectable families in the same
manner.

There was no clear distinction between private and
public, religious and secular celebrations in early Los
Angeles. The smallness of the town precluded exclu-

31. Maurice H. Newmark and Marco R. Newmark (eds.), *Sixty
Years in Southern California, 1853–1913: Containing the Reminiscences
of Harris Newmark,* p. 102.

32. Packman, *Leather Dollars,* pp. 41–42. The 12 characters represented were the infant Jesus, Mary, Joseph, El Angel, La Hilda
(St. Elizabeth), El Hermito (the Hermit), Bartolo Flojo (Bartholo-
mew the Lazy One), Caitas (Satan), El Diablo Cajo (the Lame
Devil), and Los Tres Reyes (the Three Kings). M. R. Cole, *Los Pastores: A Mexican Play of the Nativity.*

sive social or religious cliques. Celebrations of birth, baptism, adulthood, marriage, and death centered on the plaza and usually involved the whole community.

Californio Politics

The geographical isolation of Alta California gave rise to a peculiar political history during the Mexican era. Unlike some areas of central Mexico, where administrative pressures from the capital tended to dominate local government and society, California sustained a remarkable degree of self-government. The Californios were able to resist with armed force the centralist policies of the numerous governors sent from Mexico. Between 1828 and 1845 there were at least five successful revolts.

The underlying causes of these revolts were local jealousies, not disloyalty to the Mexican nation. The central government appreciated this fact—it was itself wracked by similar intrigues and pronunciamentos. In California, the Mexican government recognized the legitimacy of each succeeding rebel cause; once the rebels had won, it pardoned the victors and allowed them to continue their administrations. Since it lacked both funds and internal stability, the central government was unable to force the Californios into submission.

Rebellions had a mixed effect on the future ability of the Californios to resist outside aggression. The Alvarado insurrection in 1836 strengthened the power of the abajeños (Southern Californians) and generated resentments that clearly divided the Californios into northern and southern factions. The Micheltorena revolt in 1845 again reaffirmed the control of the abajeños and made Los Angeles the provincial capital. But it created hatreds that were fatal during the Mexican War.

Possibly the dissension of these years unified the pueblo communities, if only against each other. Lewis Coser, in his book *The Functions of Social Conflict,* has theorized that internal conflicts—such as those experienced by the Californios—often serve to define group life and reaffirm group identity. He suggests that conflict is not always destructive but can sometimes strengthen communal life, depending on the degree of consensus regarding the limits of violence.[33] This seems to be true of California politics during these years.

In any case, as the Mexican period wore on, revolt became an acceptable expression of both regional and pueblo political loyalty. As a result, legitimate authority came to have dual status. Today's governor was tomorrow's rebel, and vice versa. Californios were skeptical of any institutionalized power that claimed to be above human frailty. Effective leadership depended more upon personal reputation than upon elections. It was not unusual for otherwise respectable citizens to be jailed as traitors, only to be pardoned once they had sworn allegiance to the new authority. In 1836, for example, after the failure of a revolt against Alvarado, the leading rancheros of Los Angeles were arrested and imprisoned because they had been of the pro-Mexican-government faction in a dispute with the *norteños* over whether to declare independence. Eventually both factions worked out a compromise. There were no reprisals, and later many of those jailed became political leaders during the Mexican War. Thus the twin traditions of internal conflict and legitimate revolt became part of the fabric of Californio political life. During the American period, these traditions resulted in several bandit revolutionary movements which were supported by, or at least tolerated by, the majority of Hispano-Americanos.

Another important development during the Mexican period was the creation of a form of local government that was both populist and authoritarian. Spanish rule had created a centralized authoritarian structure dominated by the personal whims of the Viceroy and other Crown-appointed officials. Self-rule was instituted under the Mexican Constitution of 1824, which attempted to establish a rule of law and regional

33. Lewis A. Coser, *The Functions of Social Conflict,* p. 38.

autonomy based upon popular democracy as the Mexicans understood it. Thus local government, as it developed in Los Angeles, drew on both Spanish authoritarian and Mexican populist traditions. This mixed character of Mexican town government had important consequences for the future, not the least of which was the people's lack of understanding of American forms of government.

One indication of the vitality of local government in Los Angeles was the frequent shifting of political leadership. Authority was not frozen in the hands of a few during this period, but systematically distributed among the upper classes. Key positions in the pueblo government were frequently rotated. Between 1821 and 1845 only one man, Manuel Gutierrez, was re-elected to succeed himself as alcalde. Only 5 of the 31 alcaldes elected served more than one year. The majority of office-holders served single terms and then stepped down, allowing others to take over.[34]

At least three times during the 25 years after Mexican Independence the pobladores rebelled against the local government and meted out popular justice. One alcalde, José María Ávila, was deposed through mob action. In 1833 the murder of Felix Domingo resulted in the creation of a "Junta Defensora de la Segúridad Pública": a vigilante committee, formed to preserve order during the trial, which ended by acting as judge and executioner of the two accused men.[35] On another occasion, in 1844, Governor Pío Pico formed a citizen's militia to maintain public order upon the disbanding of the government's garrison. A year later there were popularly supported attempts to overthrow this unpopular governor.

American Contacts

The Californios frustrated the central government's policies in one key area: the restriction of foreign im-

34. Bancroft, *History of California*, passim.
35. Bancroft, *History of California*, vol. 3, pp. 418–419.

migration from the United States. This resulted more from refusal to carry out the laws than from disagreement with the purpose of the laws, which was to prevent another Texas episode. Prior to the 1840's, Mexico had not sought to limit foreign immigration to California; although, as in Texas, she had imposed certain conditions—mainly Catholicism, naturalization, and political loyalty—for foreign residence and land ownership. But the influx of foreigners after 1841, along with their increasing disregard of Mexican law, led to the formation of a more restrictive policy.

By 1842 the government sought to discourage American immigrants by requiring permits to enter the province. Soon the Mexican authorities gave the governor the power to prohibit immigration altogether, as well as the power to expel foreigners. By 1845 the central government passed laws prohibiting all further immigration into California. The Californios disregarded this policy and continued to welcome the newcomers with traditional hospitality. John Bidwell, the leader of an early American immigrant party, found that " . . . never was there a more hospitable and kindly people on the face of the earth than the native-born Californian."[36]

Despite their small numbers (not more than 50 in all of the Los Angeles District prior to 1840), many immigrants who settled near the pueblo soon became wealthy and influential members of the Hispanic community. One foreigner, the Scotsman Hugo Reid, came to California in the early 1820's, married a Gabrielino woman, and became a wealthy rancher. He served many years as a justice of the peace for the San Gabriel region and was generally regarded as a Mexicano. Other immigrants married daughters of upper-class Californio families and allied themselves by blood and land to the influential *gente de razón*. Lists of the landed aristocracy in Los Angeles prior to the conquest in 1847 included the families of Abel Stearns, Juan José Warner, "Don Benito" Wilson, John Temple, William Wolfskill, and Louis Vignes, all foreign immigrants who

36. Bancroft, *History of California*, vol. 4, p. 66.

had successfully assimilated themselves into Californio society.[37] The foreigners' intermarriage, together with their adoption of the native religion, customs, and language, seemed to make them at most curiosities rather than threats. In 1842 Manuel Requena, a close friend to many of the early American settlers, drew upon past experiences as he observed new immigrants passing through the pueblo on their way north: They "showed no desire to occupy the lands," he wrote. Undoubtedly his benign experiences with the earlier immigrants blinded him to the real dangers of continued immigration.[38]

In 1841 the character of overland migration from the United States changed. Settlers began to arrive in larger numbers with no intention of adopting the "foreign ways" of the native Californians. Many were imbued with sentiments of Manifest Destiny. One example of such an immigrant was Lansford Hastings, who returned to the eastern seaboard to write *The Emigrant's Guide*, intending to awaken other Americans to the wonders of California. Until 1848 and the Gold Rush, Hastings' book was a powerful influence in attracting foreigners to California and in shaping the anti-Mexican sentiments of newly arrived Anglo-Americans. Interspersed with inaccurate geographic information were comments on the life and culture of the Californios. In speaking of the Mestizos, he said: "More indomitable ignorance does not prevail among a people who make the least pretention to civilization; in truth, they are scarcely a visible grade, in the scale of intelligence, above the barbarous tribes by whom they are surrounded . . . they are the most dissolute and abandoned characters of the whole community."[39]

37. Susanna Bryant Dakin, *A Scotch Paisano: Hugo Reid's Life in California, 1832–1852.*

38. Manuel Requena to Estranjucio Barron, Jan. 14, 1842, in "Documentos para la historia de California, archivos de la familia Requena" (ms., Bancroft Library).

39. Hastings, *The Emigrant Guide,* p. 113, cited in George Weston Meldrum, "The History of the Treatment of Foreign and Minority Groups in California, 1830–1860" (Ph.D. diss.), p. 103.

The first real indication that these attitudes might result in conquest was Commodore Thomas Catesby Jones' premature takeover of Monterey in 1842. But this comic-opera episode was soon dismissed as a bad joke by Mexican officials, and it had little effect on the community's attitudes toward Anglo-Americans. After the annexation of Texas, however, Mexico began to fear for the safety of her neglected provinces. The minister of war in Mexico City notified Governor Micheltorena that conflict with the United States was imminent and that he should begin war preparations. Accordingly, the governor ordered a draft of every male between 16 and 60 and began stockpiling weapons at San Juan Bautista. Later reports of peace resulted in a general demobilization. The Californios, by now used to false alarms, returned to domestic political intrigues.

Less than a year after this episode, the abajeños ousted Micheltorena and installed the Angeleno Pío Pico as interim governor. He promptly moved the provincial capital to Los Angeles and elevated a host of Angelenos to power. Juan Bandini became secretary of state and Ygnacio del Valle treasurer (although the treasury remained in Monterey under the control of José de Castro). José Antonio Carrillo, Ygnacio Coronel, and Santiago Arqüello became justices in the new administration. Pico completed the secularization of the missions, put down several insurrections, and heard increasing rumors of impending war with the norteños.[40]

When Pico heard that Castro, the norteños' leader, was planning to take Los Angeles by force, he stirred the provincial assembly to raise a small army. Two of the three companies mustered for the defense of the city were commanded by foreigners, Don Benito Wilson and Julian Workman. They were considered loyal Mexicanos and even more loyal abajeños, despite the prospect of a future war with the Americans. News of the Bear Flag Rebellion and the capture of Monterey in early July changed this situation overnight. Soon suspi-

40. Bancroft, *History of California,* vol. 4, pp. 515–559.

cions forced foreign-born residents to flee to outlying rancheros.[41]

The outbreak of war initially unified the Californians. Castro and Pico met and issued a joint proclamation calling upon all loyal patriots to come to the defense of their patria. The tone of their proclamation reflected the changed mood of the Californios regarding foreigners: " . . . this is the most unjust aggression of late centuries undertaken by a nation which is ruled by the most unheard-of ambition. . . . [They have] formed the project of authorizing robbery without disguising it with the slightest shame. . . ."[42]

But in Los Angeles not all Mexicanos were united in their opposition to the "gringo" invaders. Twenty-five years of factional strife had left jealousies and feuds that were not easily set aside by a piece of paper. Some Angelenos suspected Castro's motives in the reconciliation with Pico, and a few refused to cooperate in giving him needed supplies. Others, mostly upper-class, who feared the patriotic elements as much as the Yankees, fled to their distant ranchos to await the outcome of the war. A few Californios even joined the American forces as they approached the pueblo from San Pedro. Most of the evidence indicates that the lower classes remained loyal and stayed to defend their homes. Among these, most of them cholos, patriotism and anti-gringo sentiments were at fever pitch.[43] Later, during the first American occupation of the town, they would find their leader in Serbulo Varela, a landless vaquero described by California historians as a "semi-outlaw."

The Mexican War in Los Angeles

On August 13, 1846, Commodore Robert F. Stockton entered Los Angeles after fighting a brief skirmish

41. James M. Guinn, "The Siege and Capture of Los Angeles, 1846," *Q. Hist. Soc. So. Calif.* pp. 47–62; and Guinn, *A History of California and an Extended History of Los Angeles and Environs,* vol. 1, pp. 141–189.

42. Bancroft, *History of California,* 1846–1848, vol. 5, p. 263.

43. *Ibid.,* p. 265.

on the outskirts of the pueblo. Once in possession of
the city, he immediately imposed martial law, forbidding public meetings and the carrying of firearms. He
then left Captain Archibald Gillespie and about 50 soldiers in charge.

Gillespie's harsh and tactless enforcement of the occupation orders soon made the Americans unpopular.
In the early-morning hours of September 22, 1846,
María Flores and Serbulo Varela led an attack on the
American garrison. By dawn the Americans had re-
treated to their stronghold on Fort Hill. During the
siege that followed, the insurgents issued *El Plan de Los
Angeles,* setting forth the reason for their actions and
calling all loyal Mexicanos to arms. Probably written
by Leonardo Cota, the "Plan," signed by many others,
expressed the fears of the pobladores regarding the
Yankee conquest. In part it read: "An insignificant
force of adventurers from the United States of North
America, which is putting us in a condition worse than
that of slaves, are dictating to us despotic and arbitrary laws, which by loading us with contributions
and onerous taxes, they wish to destroy our industries
and agriculture and compel us to abandon our property.... "[44]

This was the first written statement issued by the
Hispanic peoples of California protesting the injustices
of the American occupation. It set the tone for later
claims to redress that were to echo in the editorials of
the Spanish-language newspapers, in the addresses of political leaders, and in personal correspondence throughout the nineteenth century.

In the battles and skirmishes that took place during
the five months that the pueblo remained in Mexican
hands, the Angelenos showed their determination to
defend their homeland and way of life. The California

---

44. *El Plan de Los Angeles* can be found in English translation in
Bancroft, *History of California,* vol. 5, p. 310. The original is *Pronunciamento de Varela y otros Californios contra los Americanos* (ms., Bancroft Library); commentary on this document can be found in
Guinn, "Siege and Capture," p. 51.

lancers, using guerrilla tactics, proved that they could hold at bay a numerically superior army equipped with more advanced weapons. The Mexicans won guerilla victories at Chico Rancho (September 26 and 27, 1846), Dominguez Rancho (October 8), Natividad (November 29), and San Pasqual (December 8). They had the advantages of familiar terrain, better horses and horsemen, easy food supply, a friendly population, and bold leadership. Andrés Pico and José Carillo led the successful attacks at San Pasqual and Dominguez Rancho, but there were other guerrilla leaders. Jesús Pico, Francisco Rico, José Antonio Carrillo, Augustín Olvera, and Manual Gárfias also helped defend the pueblo as the Americans advanced.[45]

Despite the fact that the great majority of pobladores supported armed resistance, there were significant defections and divisions among the Californio leadership. This, in the end, led to their defeat. Angustias de la Guerra Ord remembered the lukewarm support members of her class gave the patriots. Others observed that most of the large landholders remained neutral throughout the conflict.[46] Animosities between the Mexican and native-born also divided the ranks of the Californios. Flores, a Mexican leader of some importance, was arrested by Pico in December 1846 and accused of disloyalty to the Californios' cause. Pico, too, was arrested briefly and held prisoner as the Americans advanced on the town. These squabbles, along with the reinforcement of the Americans by General Stephan W. Kearney, had a predictable result in the Californio capitulation at Cahuenga Pass on January 13, 1847.[47]

Ironically, defeat created unity among the Californios. Generals Flores, Castro, and Pico, along with a sizable portion of the army, departed for Mexico in disgust after the signing of the ceasefire, thus removing the most volatile elements from the pueblo. Frémont, who was the new governor, aided this unification by

45. Bancroft, *History of California,* vol. 5, pp. 403–404.
46. Ord, *Occurrences,* p. 53.
47. Bancroft, *History of California,* vol. 5, pp. 227–235.

allowing the Angelenos to continue their local government and traditional fiestas. Anxious to avoid the
mistakes of Gillespie, he dressed himself in the Californio style, surrounded himself with Californio advisors,
and even ordered the army band to give concerts in the
plaza.

But at the same time Frémont initiated a system of
forced loans from the rich. As an example, he extorted
loans from two conservative businessmen, Eulegio de
Celis and Antonio Cota, at an interest rate of 1.5 percent per month—eventually Frémont owed these two
over 500,000 dollars. Then President Buchanan re-
pudiated Frémont's transactions and cancelled his
debts. Such freebooting alienated the formerly neutral
upper classes and gave them good reason to make
common cause with the despised *cholos*. [48]

The Mexicanos of Los Angeles were further united
by the feeling that they had been betrayed and abandoned by Mexico. The Treaty of Guadalupe Hidalgo
came as a profound shock to the patriotic element.
They now suffered supreme insult at the hands of their
own country: they were sold. One observer noted the
feelings of most Mexicanos: There was "a revulsion of
feeling toward Mexico which no repentant action on
her part could ever overcome. The native people felt
that they had been sold and expressed in no measured
terms their indignation. . . ."[49]

These feelings might have given way to more violent
actions but for the cautious administration of the
American officials who made a point, during the first
months, of letting the Californios have their own way.
In February, less than a month after the end of the war,
José Salazar and Enrique Ávila were elected alcaldes in
the traditional manner. A few months later, Pío Pico
returned from Mexico and, after a brief stay in the local
jail, resumed his position as leader of the conservative
faction.

    48. Meldrum, "Treatment," pp. 286–287.
    49. Colton, *Three Years in California,* in Meldrum, "Treatment,"
pp. 357–358.

The Americans tested their strength in January 1848 by invalidating the elections of Ignacio Palomares and José Sepúlveda and appointing Stephan C. Foster as mayor. But the next year, pressure from the numerically dominant Hispano-Americanos, as they were now beginning to call themselves, succeeded in electing Vicente Guerrero and Abel Stearns, two old-line Californios.[50] When California became a state in 1850, the old forms of local government with their dual alcaldes and electoral systems were abolished. The Mexican community began a painful process of changing its traditional way of life.

50. Bancroft, *History of California,* vol. 5, p. 626.

CHAPTER TWO

Exclusion from a Developing Economy

Historians who have studied the social and economic history of the Spanish-speaking population in the southwestern United States after the Mexican War have agreed that the landholding classes were robbed of their possessions in violation of the Treaty of Guadalupe Hidalgo. As early as 1871, Henry George summarized the history of the Mexican grants in postwar California by saying that it was "a history of greed, of perjury, of corruption, of speculation and highhanded robbery for which it will be difficult to find a parallel. . . . "[1] A few years later, Herbert Howe Bancroft, commenting on the effect of the Gwin Land Act on the Californios, noted that "the law was oppressive and ruinous. . . . It was in no sense the protection promised by the treaty."[2] Successive historians such as Josiah Royce, Robert McCleland, Leonard Pitt, and others have echoed the verdicts of George and Bancroft.[3]

1. Henry George, *Our Land and Our Land Policy, National and State* (San Francisco, 1871), p. 14.
2. Bancroft, *History of California*, 1848–1859, vol. 6, pp. 576–577.
3. For citations which agree in substance with George and Bancroft, see: Josiah Royce, *California from Conquest in 1848 to the Second Vigilance Committee in San Francisco: A Study in American Character*, pp. 385–387; Pitt, *The Decline of the Californios*, pp. 110–119; Robert Glass Cleland, *The Cattle on a Thousand Hills: Southern California, 1850–1880*, pp. 49–50; Albert Prago, *Strangers in Their Own Land: A History of Mexican-Americans*, pp. 113–114; Matt S. Meier

More recently, Rudolfo Acuña has given a Chicano historian's view on this issue. For him, the Anglos acted as imperial colonizers who systematically exploited, brutalized, and oppressed the native population, much as the Europeans were to do later in nineteenth-century Africa and Asia. The treatment of the Californio landholders was part of the larger historical process of colonization of nonwhite peoples.[4]

This general thesis, developed over 90 years of California historiography, will be put to the test of quantitative evidence in this chapter. I have chosen to approach the problem by analyzing the degree to which members of La Raza were excluded from the economic development of the pueblo of Los Angeles after the American takeover.

The Spanish-speaking Californians, who lost their lands after 1848, were members of a landed minority. This elite comprised no more than 3 percent of a total mixed Mexican and Indian population of just under 10,000. In this light, it is important to ask whether or not there was an overall economic and demographic decline, not only among the property-holders, but among all members of the pueblo in terms of occupational mobility and opportunity.

If those who lost their lands transferred their wealth to other endeavors, such as commerce and industry, and if the general population experienced an overall growth and economic improvement, defined as moving from manual to white-collar occupations, then we can qualify the thesis of economic decline. If, on the other hand, in addition to the elite's loss of land, the Mexican-American population underwent a demographic decline and was shut out of an expanding

---

and Feliciano Rivera, *The Chicanos, A History of Mexican-Americans*, p. 191; David J. Weber (ed.), *Foreigners in Their Native Land: Historical Roots of the Mexican-Americans*, p. 158; McWilliams, *North from Mexico*, pp. 88–94.

4. Rudolfo Acuña, *Occupied America: The Chicano's Struggle Toward Liberation*, pp. 1–5.

economy, then this would provide support for the thesis of stagnation.

In all this there is a need to refine our understanding of the economic and social history of Spanish-speaking nineteenth-century California and to move beyond class-determined generalizations. Some younger scholars are already doing this. Charles Hughes has accounted for the economic decline of the landed gentry in San Diego County by pointing to the underdeveloped state of the ranching economy resulting from constant Indian depredations.[5] Mario García, also researching the economic history of the Californios in San Diego, has determined that political exclusion played an important part in hastening their economic decline.[6] No doubt specific historical, political, and demographic considerations in each community should be examined to give an accurate picture of the complexity of the transformation of Spanish-speaking California's pastoral economy.

During the American era, the pueblo of Los Angeles began to experience the problems and benefits associated with rapid modernization. The development of small-scale industry, intensive commercial farming, and technological innovation introduced a new kind of urban society at odds with the traditional Californio way of life.

Contrasting the city as it was in the early 1850's with its economic development thirty years later illustrates the rapidity of this growth. The population grew from 1,610 residents in 1850 to over 11,183 in 1880 (see Table 3). This increase in population, along with improvements in transportation, created a new market economy and altered the older occupational system. To feed a growing population, more and more land came under the plow; by 1880 farm acreage had increased

5. Charles Hughes, "The Decline of the Californios: The Case of San Diego, 1846–1856," *J. San Diego Hist.*

6. Mario García, "The Californios of San Diego and the Politics of Accommodation," *Aztlán.*

100 times over what it had been in 1850.[7] In 1850 the census-taker had counted only one factory, a bakery employing two men; by 1880 there were over 117 industrial establishments employing over 700 workers.[8]

Los Angeles did not become a major industrial center, however. The growth of commercial farming and trading was more important, as was the development of public works. The city built a potable water system, a sewage system, a gasworks, a telegraph system, railroad connections, and a network of paved public roads. Public-works construction, in turn, increased the value of the land and attracted more settlers. As a result, property values rose to an assessed valuation of over twenty million dollars by 1880.[9]

Most estimates of Los Angeles' population growth after the Mexican War have been based on the decennial United States censuses. While there are good reasons for regarding these government documents with suspicion, they are still more reliable than estimates based on other sources such as diaries or city directories. But for the Bureau of the Census, La Raza poses a special problem. Until 1930, the Bureau did not separate Mexican-American statistics from those for the general population. Historians have been forced to define their own categories, review the original returns, and reconstruct a census summary. Some of the procedures and sources I have used in drawing statistically based conclusions about the Californio population are discussed in Appendix A.

Evidence available from these census sources indicates that the Anglo-Americans became a numerical

7. Robert Fogelson, *The Fragmented Metropolis: Los Angeles, 1850–1930*, p. 67, Table 2.

8. Maurice H. Newmark and Marco R. Newmark, *The Census of Los Angeles, 1850*, p. 118; U.S. Department of the Interior, Bureau of the Census, *Compendium of the Tenth Census (June 1, 1880)*, p. 947.

9. Guinn, *A History of California and an Extended History of Los Angeles and Environs*, vol. 1, p. 254.

majority in the city after 1860. Until then the Spanish-speaking outnumbered the Anglo-Americans in the pueblo (see Table 3). Between 1850 and 1860, the Mexican-American population increased by about 800 persons while the Anglo population increased by more than 1,900. Between 1860 and 1880, the Mexican-American population stabilized at about 2,100 while the Anglo population continued to grow.

Why did the Spanish-speaking population cease to grow after 1860? To some extent this apparent stabilization of the population may be explained by errors in census reporting. There is some basis for the belief that undercounting in the census was a constant source of miscalculation. But if we allow for the same percentage of error in each census year, we are still left with the general trends of growth and stabilization.[10] This demographic pattern may be explained by reference to four factors: the birthrate, the deathrate, immigration, and emigration. Ultimately all of these factors were related to one another and to socioeconomic conditions.

The Mexican-American birthrate rose until about 1865, when it began to decline. The absence of reliable statistics on mortality prior to 1870 makes it difficult to generalize about the relationship between births and increases. It is interesting to note, however, that the trends in births and population were parallel. That is, after a period of growth prior to 1860, both population and the birthrate stabilized.

An analysis of the migration of Spanish-speaking

10. Peter Knights has found that in Boston (1860–1890) the census consistently underenumerated about 9 percent of the real population. His method was to check the census returns against city directory information and impressionistic sources. Since no city directories for Los Angeles were published until 1872, that method is impractical for this study. Based on Knights' findings, however, we may be warranted in the assumption that the percentage of error, whatever it was, remained consistent, and that the gross trends of occupational and economic changes remained unaffected by the incompleteness of the data. See Peter R. Knights, "A Method for Estimating Census Under-Enumeration," *Hist. Methods Newsletter*, pp. 6–7.

TABLE 3

Population Growth and Stabilization in
Los Angeles, 1850–1880

	1850[a]	1860	1870	1880
Total city population[b]	1,610	4,385	5,728	11,183
Mexican-American population[c]	1,215	2,069	2,160	2,166
Mexican-American proportion of city population	75.4%	47.1%	37.7%	19.3%

a. Some controversy surrounds the accuracy of the 1850 census. For a brief description of the rationale for using this document rather than the 1852 State Census, see Appendix A, Part 4.

b. U.S. Dept. of Commerce, Bureau of the Census, *Fifteenth Census of the United States*, "Population," 1 (1931): 18–19; De Bow, Bureau of the Census, *Statistical View of the United States . . . Being a Compendium of the Seventh Census* (1854): 202.

c. For an explanation of the computer analysis of manuscript returns, see Appendix A.

persons, either foreign-born or those born in other parts of the United States, shows how many persons were added to or lost from the population. The results of these computations for migratory population changes are presented in Table 4.

An analysis of the stable Spanish-speaking population which remained in the city between censuses can be used to check the reliability of the migration trends described in Table 4. If few Spanish-speaking people remained in the pueblo between census years, then it would be correct to assume that there was a good deal of migration. Computing the persistence rate would enable us to judge how important migration trends were in relation to the numbers added through natural increase: a high persistence rate would suggest that most of the increase among native Californians was due to fluctuations in births and deaths.

TABLE 4
Migratory Population Changes,
1844–1880[a]

	1844–1860	1860–1880
Net population increase	1,105	−333
Non-native California increase:		
Net immigration	410	39
Net emigration	−12	−226
Native increase	707	−107

SOURCE: Computer analysis of manuscript census returns (see Appendix A).

a. This table excludes increases due to births and deaths. It measures only net, not total, increases and decreases, and does not show year-by-year fluctuations. Since reliable information on yearly population changes is lacking (city directories were not published until 1872, and were generally less reliable than the census), we are forced to use the decennial information.

We can use this information to compare the Mexican-American population of Los Angeles with the general populations of other cities. As can be seen from Table 5, the Los Angeles Spanish-speaking had a low rate of persistence in comparison to the populations of other United States cities, particularly after 1860.[11] The

11. Some historians have developed computer programs to trace persisting individuals over time. This is called "linking records." See M. H. Skolnich, "A Computer Program for Linking Records," *Hist. Meth. Newsletter;* H. B. Newcombe, "Record Linking: The Design for Linking Records into Individual and Family Histories," *Am. J. Human Genetics;* and Ian Winchester, "The Linkage of Historical Records by Man and Computer Techniques and Problems," *J. Inter-Disciplinary Hist.* Unfortunately it was not possible to use a computer to link records in this study, due to the many ambiguities in the spellings of last names and inaccuracies in the census reporting. The procedure I have followed instead was to first alphabetize the 9,000 or more census records and then—taking into account variant spellings and keypunch errors—link, by hand, those persisting records. Later, through the use of an SPSS computer program, I grouped the persisting individuals into discrete categories according

TABLE 5

Comparative Persistence Rates for Los Angeles
Mexican-Americans and Selected Urban Communities

Decade	Location	Persistence rate[a] (expressed as a percentage)
1850–1860	Los Angeles	
	Mexican-Americans	28
	Boston	39
	Philadelphia	32
	Waltham, Mass.	44
	Northampton, Mass.	53
1860–1870	Los Angeles	
	Mexican-Americans	11
	Poughkeepsie, N.Y.	49
	Waltham, Mass.	45
1870–1880	Los Angeles	
	Mexican-Americans	11
	Waltham, Mass.	50
	Poughkeepsie, N.Y.	50
	Atlanta, Ga.	44
	San Antonio, Texas	32
	San Francisco	48

SOURCE: Data for selected urban communities other than Los Angeles was compiled by Stephen Thernstrom in *The Other Bostonians: Poverty and Progress in the American Metropolis,* pp. 222–223. Data for Los Angeles Mexican-Americans was drawn from a computer analysis of manuscript census returns.

a. Ratio of male heads of households persisting to the end of the period to the total number of male heads of households at the beginning of the period.

to the length of time they continued to live in the city. The persisting sample included heads of households, property-owning adults, children who came of age during the period (21 years), and propertyless adults. Males and females were included in all groups. Nevertheless, the sample is still probably low, since it did not include children who did not come of age in the period and women who, through marriage, changed their surnames.

relatively high persistence rate prior to this date was probably due to the economic prosperity of that era, which induced people to stay in the pueblo.

Looking at the entire period from 1844 to 1880, we get another picture of population movement: only 12 heads of households who lived in the city in 1844 remained until 1880. An additional 10 persisted from 1850 to 1880.[12] From this it appears that for the Spanish-speaking, migration was a main source of population change.[13]

The Spanish-speaking of Los Angeles were geographically mobile. Prior to 1852, most of the new Mexican immigrants to California came from Sonora and other northern Mexican states. The ferryman at the Yuma crossing, Dr. Lincoln, reckoned that between 1848 and 1852 almost 25,000 Mexican immigrants from Sonora crossed into California on their way to the gold fields.[14] Many of these immigrants brought their families and stayed.

12. A matrix of the numbers in persisting households for Los Angeles is as follows:

| First year listed in census | 1844 | Last Year Listed in Census | | | |
		1850	1860	1870	1880
1844		28	52	17	12
1850			49	15	10
1860				44	39
1870					38

13. For a more detailed study of immigration from Mexico, see Doris M. Wright, "The Making of Cosmopolitan California: An Analysis of Immigration, 1848–1870," *Calif. Hist. Q.*; and Allyn C. Loosley, *The Foreign-Born Population of California, 1848–1920.*

14. Evidence regarding population movements between Mexico and the United States during the nineteenth century are fragmentary and generally unreliable. For a full discussion of the many problems involved, see Leo Grebler's *The Mexican Immigration to the United States: The Record and Its Implications,* pp. 17–19.

Several researchers have pieced together fragments of information to give us an idea of the magnitude of the population movement between the two countries. Richard Lee Nostrand, in "The Hispanic-American Borderlands: A Regional Historical Geog-

In the course of the 1850's, political and social discrimination and violence drove many Mexican immigrants out of the gold fields. Some made their way into the southern counties.[15] Census data for Los Angeles indicate that Mexican miners and immigrants played an important part in changing the social composition of the pueblo. By 1860 the Mexican-born population of the city was five times as large as it had been in 1844. After 1870 the Mexican-born percentage dropped, paralleling a decline in Mexican immigration (see Table 6). By 1880, more than 90 percent of the total population had migrated there after the Mexican War of 1848.[16]

raphy" (Ph.D. diss.), estimated that the total number of Mexican immigrants to the Southwest for the period 1820–1900 was 54,000. This estimate was based for the most part on Bancroft's *History of California*, but also on Elizabeth Broadbent's work, "The Distribution of the Mexican Population in the United States" (Master's thesis). Broadbent estimated (Table 1, p. 4) that for the period 1850–1900, Mexican immigration was as follows:

Year	Mexican-Born Residents of the Southwest
1850	13,317
1860	27,466
1870	42,435
1880	68,399
1890	77,853
1900	103,393

Based on her computations, it would seem that over 90,000 Mexican-born immigrants came into the United States Southwest between 1850 and 1900.

Another methodology for estimating the size of the Spanish-speaking population in the Southwest during the nineteenth century has been advanced by Oscar Martinez in "On the Size of the Chicano Population: New Estimates, 1850–1890," *Aztlán*. He calculates an upper and lower range population estimate taking into account the probability of a 40 percent error in underenumeration. He also critically evaluates previous estimates made by Bancroft and other historians.

15. Pitt, *Decline*, pp. 63–64. See also his "The Beginnings of Nativism in California," *Pac. Hist. Rev.*

16. One indication of a high transiency rate among Mexican-Americans comes from a comparison of the 1850 federal census

TABLE 6

The Mexican-Born Population of Los Angeles,
1844–1880

	1844	1850	1860	1870	1880
Total Spanish-speaking population	1,469	1,215	2,069	2,160	2,166
Mexican-born	135	242	640	615	438
Mexican-born as a proportion of total population	9.2%	19.9%	30.9%	28.5%	10.9%

SOURCE: Computer analysis of manuscript census returns.

That most of the Mexicans who migrated to Los
Angeles came from Sonora is evidenced by the name
the Anglo-American residents gave the Spanish-
speaking section: Sonora Town. Numerous firsthand
accounts of frontier violence in Los Angeles during the

---

with the 1852 state census (see Appendix A). The state census
counted 914 more white persons (including Mexican-Americans
and Anglos) than the federal census. This indicated that in only two
years almost 1,000 migrants entered the city (excluding the natural
increase, which was negligible). I searched the state census, which
was not divided into city and county populations as was the federal
census, and located certain families which had been listed two years
earlier. I found that most of the families listed in 1850 had disappeared. Further checking the consecutive order of the state census
listings (assuming that the census-taker had proceeded door to door
and street by street), I found that those Mexican-American families
that did remain in the pueblo either moved or experienced drastic
changes in their family composition. For example, in 1850 José de
Jesus and Julian de Largo had lived with the Celis family. Two
years later they were no longer living with this family. The Celises
now had two new neighbors—John B. Lewis and M. B. Alanis.
The Bochet family also continued to live in the pueblo during the
two censuses; within two years they moved to another region of
the city. Another persisting family was the Coronels. In two years
the Coronel household increased by 9 members: 6 were Indian servants, and 3 were probably visiting travelers or boarders.

1850's also indicate something of the social impact of this immigration. Many Anglo-American gold miners stopped off in Sonora Town, and much of the crime and violence of this era was due to their explosive mixture with the new arrivals from Mexico.[17]

In general, the three decades after the end of the Mexican War were a time of demographic instability. A major social influence was the transiency of the population, as seen in the declining rate of persistence in each census year. These changes broke the continuity of traditional pueblo life.

Socioeconomic Changes

It is not surprising to find that these demographic patterns can be correlated with economic fluctuations. Spanish-speaking immigrants were attracted to Los Angeles during times of prosperity, and left during periods of economic depression. In general, men and women married younger and began families sooner when times were good. When times were bad, they delayed marriage and children.

During the early period of population growth (1850–1860), the rancheros of southern California prospered. An increased demand for beef in the northern gold fields throughout the 1850's resulted in high cattle prices.[18] According to Judge Benjamin Hayes,

17. Vivid accounts of Sonora Town in the 1850's can be found in Bell, *Reminiscences of a Ranger,* p. 36; Newmark and Newmark (eds.), *Sixty Years in Southern California,* pp. 135–166; and Pitt, *Decline,* ch. 9.

18. W. W. Robinson, *Los Angeles from the Days of the Pueblo,* p. 52. Los Angeles' economic history in the nineteenth century has been thoroughly documented by numerous historians. The earliest, and from many standpoints the best, is *A History of Los Angeles County California with Illustrations* written by Thomas H. Thompson, Augustus West, and J. Albert Wilson and published in Los Angeles in 1880. The best contemporary economic histories of this period are Remi A. Nadeau, *City Makers: The Men Who Transformed Los Angeles from a Village to a Metropolis During the First Great Boom, 1868–1876;* Fogelson, *The Fragmented Metropolis;* and Max Vorspan and Lloyd P. Gartner, *A History of the Jews in Los Angeles.*

about three-fifths of the cattle in Los Angeles County at that time belonged to native Californios.[19] Cattle could be sold in San Francisco for 50 to 60 dollars a head; it cost the Southern Californians 15 to 20 dollars to raise and transport a steer to the northern market. Between 1851 and 1856, they drove more than 55,000 head north to feed the hundreds of thousands of newly arrived gold miners. In this way some of the prosperity of the decade filtered down into the hands of Mexican-American Angelenos.

The cattle boom ended abruptly in the early 1860's. Between January 1862 and March 1864, only four inches of rain fell in Southern California; more than 50,000 head of cattle died of starvation during the dry spell. By 1864, cattle driven overland from the midwestern United States were of higher quality than the California animals. At about the same time, the immigration of gold seekers declined. The price of California cattle fell to about 37½ cents a head in Santa Barbara. Then in 1865 a cattle epidemic swept through the southern counties. By 1870 only about 13,000 head remained of the more than 100,000 animals that had once roamed the hills.[20]

As if these natural disasters were not enough, the Californio landholders were set upon by tax collectors, squatters, loan sharks, lawyers, and politicians. In 1851 Senator William M. Gwin, responding to pressure from Anglo-American squatters, pushed through a bill establishing a land commission charged with validating Mexican land grants in California. The basic assumption of the Gwin Bill was that most grants were illegal and that the burden of proof rested upon the California hacendados. This law violated specific provisions of the Treaty of Guadalupe Hidalgo, namely Articles VIII and IX, which guaranteed the property rights of Mexican citizens.[21]

19. Thompson, West, and Wilson, *A History of Los Angeles County*, pp. 57–58.

20. Cleland, *Cattle on a Thousand Hills*, p. 135.

21. Wayne Moquin and Charles Van Doren (eds.), *A Documentary History of the Mexican-Americans*, p. 185.

Photo.
By Godfrey

3. A panoramic view of Sonora Town taken by William Godfrey
about 1870. Courtesy of the Los Angeles Museum of Natural History.

4. Adobe brick-making. Most of the Sonora Town homes built in the nineteenth century continued to be made in the traditional manner. Courtesy of the California Historical Society, Los Angeles.

The fact that state government questioned the validity of all land titles in California encouraged squatters to move in and hire lawyers to prosecute spurious claims to the land. During the period of title indeterminacy, there was almost constant warfare between the squatters and the rancheros. Murders, mob violence, lynchings, and intimidations of all sorts on the part of the Anglo-American squatters were common occurrences throughout California, especially in the north where land was more valuable and Anglos more numerous.[22]

In the south, the hacendados were able to hold their own until the disastrous weather of 1863–64. The rapid fall in cattle prices forced many Californios to sell their lands to pay legal fees, taxes, and loan interest. Many had contracted debts at exorbitant rates of interest in order to meet their obligations during the drought. John G. Downey, for example, lent out money to Californios at 5 percent compounded monthly;[23] interest rates as high as 10 percent per month were not unusual. In order to pay back these loans, the Californios were forced to sell their lands to speculators, often before their title had been confirmed in the courts.[24]

Those who refused to contract loans lost their property at sheriffs' auctions for back taxes. During the 1850's, the property tax rate rose to about 10 cents per assessed 100 dollars valuation.[25] To pay these high taxes, Julio Verdugo had mortgaged his Rancho San Rafael (36,403 acres) to Jacob Elias for 3,445 dollars at 3

22. Pitt, *Decline,* chs. 5, 9, and 12.
23. Albert Lucian Lewis, "Los Angeles in the Civil War Decades, 1850–1868" (Ph.D. diss.), p. 20.
24. One such speculator was A. Martinore, who combed the state hiring Mexican real estate agents to advise him of those families who were ready to sell. Martinore wrote to one such agent, Juan de Toro, sometime in the early 'sixties: "I know there are many properties for sale. You see the owners and arrange with them. You know all those persons. It is necessary for you to explain everything to them and they must understand our conditions." A. Martinore to Juan de Toro, n.d. (Letter 7, DE 831, Coronel Collection, L. A. County Mus. Nat. Hist.)
25. Bancroft, *History of California,* vol. 6, pp. 613–616.

percent per month, payable quarterly. After eight years, this debt was about 58,000 dollars and Verdugo was forced to sell his entire rancho to Alfred B. Chapman. Out of pity, Chapman gave old Verdugo twenty acres to live on. Other Californios who lost their lands in this way were not as lucky.[26]

From a quantitative point of view, the economic history of Mexican-Americans in Los Angeles reveals significant variations from the fate of the rural Californios. The Spanish-speaking within the city limits were relatively unaffected by the prosperity of the 'fifties, at least in terms of the number of heads of families owning property. During the 1850's—a period of population growth—the percentage of heads of families holding land greatly decreased (see Table 7). This suggests a trend toward a concentration of wealth within the community.

In 1850, 61 percent of Mexican-American heads of families owned small parcels of land worth more than 100 dollars. The average holding per family head was worth about 2,100 dollars. By 1860, however, several years before the cattle depression, the percentage of property-holding family heads had dwindled by more than half—by then only about 29 percent of the Mexican-American population owned land. At the same time the average value of holdings decreased, so that by 1860 the median value of property held was about 1,200 dollars. This decline in property values continued in the next decade, so that by 1870 less than one-quarter of all heads of households owned property, and that was worth about half the value of the property owned in 1850.

This new data revises the traditional view that the Spanish-speaking in Southern California lost their land

26. W. W. Robinson, *The Lawyers of Los Angeles*, p. 64.

27. This view that the economic decline in terms of property-holding was delayed in Southern California can be found in the following works: Pitt, *Decline*, p. 91; Acuña, *Occupied America*, p. 106; McWilliams, *North from Mexico*, p. 92; Meier and Rivera, *The Chicanos*, pp. 82–83.

TABLE 7

Mexican-American Property-Holders in Los Angeles,
1850–1870

Year	Number of property-holding heads of families	Number of families	Percentage of family heads holding property	Average value of property
1850	135	220	61.4%	$2,105
1860	153	530	28.8	1,228
1870	116	545	21.2	1,072

SOURCE: Computer analysis of manuscript census returns.

only after the 1862 drought and depression.[27] It is evident that the process of property disenfranchisement was well underway before the 1860's. From this it appears that the economic fortunes of the Angelenos followed a different trajectory from that of the landholders in the surrounding countryside. This discrepancy may have been due to the rapid pace of commercial activity prevalent in the pueblo. There was simply more pressure exerted on Mexican-American landholders within the city limits, where land was more valuable, than in the rural areas. Speculators, lawyers, and investors were naturally more anxious to obtain title to land in the growing city than they were to acquire remote parcels.

This explanation seems to make sense when we examine the economic fortunes of the persisting property-holders in the pueblo. By the 1860's, there were more Mexican-Americans who owned property than there had been in 1850. Who were these new landholders? Did they represent an accretion to the Californio elite or were they an entirely new property-holding class? Table 8 summarizes the data for Mexican-Americans who continued to own property in the city.

The Spanish-speaking population of Los Angeles exhibited a low rate of property retention. Only about

TABLE 8

Persisting Property-Holders in Selected Periods

Period	Number of property-holding heads of families at beginning of period (1)	Number of property-holding heads of families at end of period (2)	Percentage (2/1)
1850–1870[a]	135	0	0%
1850–1860	135	15	11
1860–1870	153	7	5
1876–1886[b]	166[c]	27	23

a. This computer analysis of manuscript census returns does not count those Mexican-Americans who inherited land upon the death of a parent or spouse. The property records do not provide information on inheritance. Thus this count is low.

Further, this data does not reveal the continued ownership of a given parcel of land by a given individual, but only land-owning status. During these decades, Mexican-Americans could and did sell their lands only to buy other, usually smaller, parcels. Thus they continued to be counted as persisting property-holders, even though they no longer owned their original lands.

b. Based on computer analysis of assessment books for 1876, 1885, and 1886. *Assessment Book for the Property of Los Angeles County for the Year 1885, City,* vol. 118; *Assessment Book 1886, City,* vols. 8, 9; and *Assessment Book for the Property of Los Angeles County for the Year 1876, City* (in the L.A. County Mus. Nat. Hist.). The lists for 1885 and 1886 are incomplete.

c. Estimate based on 1870 census.

one-tenth of all Mexican-American landholders in 1850 continued to own property within the city limits in the period 1850–1860. It may have been that those who left the city sold out to purchase property elsewhere, but this is almost impossible to verify. But we can reconstruct a social profile of landholders who continued to live in Los Angeles. In the 1850's, they tended to be the older Mexican or California-born who had taken advantage of the cattle boom and become ranchers. These were men whose affluence enabled them to support their relatives within their households. During the decade they increased the amount and value of their holdings.

After 1860 there was a noticeable decline in property-holding persistence. Only 5 percent of all Mexican-American landholders in 1860 continued to hold property during this decade. The reason is not hard to discern: the 'sixties were punctuated with depression and declining cattle prices as well as with increasing taxes. Of those who continued to own property in the period 1860–1870, most were old men born in Mexico who had been recent immigrants to the city. The majority were not ranchers but merchants, professionals, and laborers who had managed to acquire a parcel of land.

In the years after 1870, the persistence rate for Mexican-American landholders rose to 23 percent. This suggests an improvement in the conditions determining land ownership for the Spanish-speaking after 1870. The prosperity induced by the coming of the railroad in 1876 may have accounted for this improvement.

By 1880, those Mexican-American families who owned property were new to the city—they had not been residents prior to 1850. They were a newly propertied class, not the remnants of an older Californio order. The traditional view of the Californios desperately trying to hold on to their lands needs to be revised in light of the experience of the landholders of Los Angeles. Mexican-Americans were caught in the revolving door of speculation, buying and selling land usually within a ten-year period. The point made by the data on persisting landholders, however, is that it was not only the Anglos who took over the Californio lands. There were also landless Mexican-Americans who acquired property through the pressure of adverse economic conditions, only to lose this newly purchased land within a short time.[28] In terms of the total

28. It seems to have been a practice for members of the same family to sell one another land at token prices, either to avoid in-

TABLE 9
Social Characteristics of Persisting Property-Owners

Category	1850–1860 Number persisting	1850–1860 Percentage	1860–1870 Number persisting	1860–1870 Percentage
Age at beginning of period:				
51–60	15	100%		
61–over			7	100%
Place of birth:				
Mexico	7	47	5	71
California	6	40	2	29
Other	2	13		
Family of residence at beginning of period:				
Extended	8	53	3	57
Nuclear	7	47	4	43
Family of residence at end of period:				
Extended	12	80	2	29
Nuclear	2	13	3	42
Single	1	7	2	29
Occupation at beginning of period:				
Farmer–rancher	6	40	3	43
Merchant	2	13		
Skilled			1	14
Laborer	4	27	1	14
None listed	3	20	2	29
Occupation at end of period:				
Farmer–rancher	8	53	2	29
Merchant	1	7		
Professional			1	14
Skilled	1	7		
Laborer	3	20	2	29
None listed	2	13	2	29

TABLE 9
Social Characteristics of Persisting Property-Owners
(continued)

Category	1850–1860 Number persisting	1850–1860 Percent-age	1860–1870 Number persisting	1860–1870 Percent-age
Value of property at beginning of period:				
$ 1– 100	1	7	1	14
$ 101– 500	6	40	3	43
$ 501–1000	3	20	1	14
$1001–5000	3	20	1	14
over $5000	2	13	1	14
Value of property at end of period:				
$ 101– 500	4	27	2	29
$ 501–1000	2	13	2	29
$1001–5000	5	33	1	14
over $5000	4	27	2	29

SOURCE: Computer analysis of manuscript census returns.

NOTE: Family types are defined as follows: Nuclear = husband and wife with or without children living in the same household without relatives, or a single parent with children; Extended = spouses, with or without children, with relatives; Single = unmarried individuals living alone or together in the same household.

Spanish-speaking population, fewer and fewer individuals were able to enter the landowning class and stay there.

Occupational Mobility

Changes in land ownership and retention affected a relatively small number of Mexican-Americans. Transformations in the occupational structure had greater

---

heritance and property taxes or to complicate legal proceedings so as to prolong family ownership. For example, in 1872 Andrés Machado sold 40 acres to one son for one dollar; two parcels of 100 and 1000 acres to another son for one dollar; 6 parcels of 100 and 1000 acres to another for one dollar; and 100 acres to a relative for one dollar. *La Crónica*, July 13, 1872.

implications for the economic well-being of the Spanish-speaking community. In Los Angeles after 1850, jobs became specialized and diversified, reflecting increasing urbanization and commercial development. To some extent, variations in the occupational structure were also due to the broader demographic and economic changes that have already been discussed. But even more important were social attitudes: those of the Mexican-Americans themselves, and those of the Anglo majority toward the Spanish-speaking. The social customs of the Hispanic community, as well as segregation and discrimination, had an influence on the types of job opportunities that were available.

Given the highly individualistic nature of the Mexican prestige system as it evolved in the Southwest, it is difficult to reconstruct a hierarchy of occupations. It is, however, possible to take some of these non-economic factors into account in the reconstruction of a Mexican-American occupational classification.

I have grouped Mexican-American occupations into five categories. At the top were the rancheros. Well into the American era, regardless of their real economic fortune, they continued to be respected by the local community, both Anglo and Spanish-speaking. Next in occupational rank were the professionals: government officials, lawyers, doctors, teachers, priests and nuns. They too had high status, owing to their specialized education and because they did not work with their hands. As with the rancheros, their position as intermediaries with the Anglo-American community conferred high status.

Next were the commercial occupations—small merchants and craftsmen who owned their own businesses. Despite their wealth, the mercantile class probably had less status in the barrio than either the ranchero or professional classes. The Hidalgo tradition of nonmanual labor, the brief history of the existence of a shop-owning class within the pueblo, and the fact that most members of that class were new to Los Angeles contributed to their relatively low social standing.

TABLE 10

Occupational Structure Among
Los Angeles Mexican-Americans,
1844–1880

	1844	1850	1860	1870	1880
Total Mexican-American work force	373	224	614	444	553
Manual laborers					
N	272	119	382	355	329
Percentage	73%	53%	62%	80%	59%
Skilled workers					
N	37	26	149	18	104
Percentage	10%	11%	24%	4%	18%
Mercantile					
N	15	23	31	16	44
Percentage	4%	10%	5%	4%	8%
Professional					
N	2	5	9	12	22
Percentage	.5%	2%	1%	2%	4%
Ranchers and farmers					
N	47	51	44	38	54
Percentage	12%	24%	8%	10%	11%

SOURCE: Computer analysis of manuscript census returns.

The laborers, skilled and unskilled—by far the most numerous members of the community—were at the bottom of the occupational pyramid because they lacked property, money, education, and influence.[29]

Table 10 presents a summary of occupational change

29. The exceedingly complex and difficult task of constructing a socioeconomic hierarchy for occupations is recognized by a number of social historians. Stephen Thernstrom, in *The Other Bostonians,* has devoted a lengthy appendix to the problem (Appendix B); Stewart Blumin, "Residential and Occupational Mobility in Antebellum Philadelphia," in Edward Pessen (ed.), *Three Centuries of*

within the Mexican-American community for the period 1844–1880. Undoubtedly the exaggerated increase in the work force in the 'fifties was due to immigration caused by favorable economic conditions. Similarly, the decline in Mexican-American employment in the 'sixties reflected the effect of economic depression and an increasingly hostile social and political environment. During the last decade, 1870–1880, employment seems to have become more stabilized, as did the general population.

The stereotypic notion that all Mexicans in the Southwest were reduced to laborers after the Mexican War is not supported by the data on occupations. The occupational distribution changed very little between 1844 and 1880. In 1844, almost 73 percent of the employed Mexican-Americans worked as unskilled laborers. With the exception of the early 1870's, there was a decline in the percentage of Spanish-speaking laborers relative to the total work force. What is more, a slightly higher percentage entered skilled and professional occupations. This same pattern of relatively unchanging occupational distribution has been noted for the Irish and German immigrants in Philadelphia for the same period, which may suggest that occupational opportunities for recent immigrants and Mexican-Americans did not change very much in the late nineteenth century.[30]

Social Mobility in America, has given considerable discussion to the matter.

Neither Thernstrom's nor Blumin's occupational hierarchy was adaptable for this study of Los Angeles, as their occupational categories were based on an urban-industrial model. This study called for a hierarchy that would take into account the transitional nature of Los Angeles' economy in these years and the pastoral and Latin values regarding manual labor in the Latin-American cultural orientation; ranching and farming were high-status occupations for the Spanish-speaking. For a fuller discussion of the rationale used in ranking occupations, see Appendix B.

30. Bruce Laurie, Theodore Hershberg, and George Alter, "Immigrants and Industry: The Philadelphia Experience, 1850–1880," *J. Soc. Hist.*

5. A Mexicano family with Gabrielino relatives resting under a *jacal*. Courtesy of Security Pacific Bank, Los Angeles.

6. A merchant and his family in front of their store on Aliso Street, 1880. Courtesy of the California Historical Society, Los Angeles.

Although the Mexican-American work force more than doubled during the early American period (1850–1880), the percentage of Mexican-American ranchers, farmers, professionals, and shop-owners declined. The decreasing importance of the landed and commercial upper classes may have been more precipitous than can be inferred from the census statistics, since the 1850 census probably undercounted the pueblo's population (see Appendix A). Initially (1844–1850), there seems to have been a brief improvement in the prospects of the upper classes. This may be accounted for in part by the inaccuracy of the 1844 census, but it is more probably related to the cattle and merchandizing boom of the early Gold Rush. The single possible exception to this view of general decline of the upper classes is a pattern of increasing Mexican-American representation in the professional occupations. But in terms of the total work force, the increase of Spanish-speaking professionals in the three decades at issue was so small as to be negligible.

To see something of the ways in which American domination affected the occupational craft structure of Los Angeles, it is useful to study those occupations which persisted from the Mexican to the American era. At least seven skilled trades that had been important during the rancho period continued to exist after 1850. Some of these occupations even expanded their employment of Mexican-Americans—this was true of such jobs as baker, blacksmith, and carpenter. Other skilled occupations passed into American hands: hat-makers, masons, and tailors ceased to number the Spanish-speaking in their ranks. Table 11 presents more detailed data for these occupations.

One possible explanation of the conflicting trends in occupational growth and decline in these traditional occupations may be found in the operations of the new market economy. Those occupations which prospered, at least among Mexican-Americans, had not yet been industrialized. Bakers and blacksmiths marketed their services directly to the pueblo population and required

TABLE 11
*Mexican-Americans Employed in
Traditional Skilled Occupations,
1844–1880*

Occupation[a]	1844	1850	1860	1870	1880
Baker	1	4	3	1	7
Blacksmith	4	3	15	1	7
Carpenter	3	7	15	2	14
Hatmaker	3	2	6	0	0
Mason	4	1	1	0	0
Tailor	3	7	0	3	0

SOURCE: Computer analysis of manuscript census returns.
a. Occupations existing in 1844 which continued into the
American era.

a minimum of credit or capital investment. On the
other hand, most of the occupations which declined or
died out among the Spanish-speaking tended to be
those which were becoming more mechanized. Thus
Mexican-American hatmakers, shoemakers, and cigar-
makers gradually disappeared under the pressure of
eastern manufactured goods. As the Mexican-American
community became less affluent, and as manufactured
goods became cheaper than hand-crafted products, demand for the latter fell off.

The degree to which Mexican-Americans participated in the commercial and industrial growth of the
city can be measured in a more positive way—namely,
through their employment in new occupations. During
the three decades after the Mexican War, over 68 new
occupations emerged, most of them in small manu-
facturing. By 1880, a few members of La Raza could
be found as cabinetmakers, soapmakers, tanners, brick-
makers, and harnessmakers—occupations which were
not listed in the pueblo census of 1844. Many also entered
new unskilled occupations as laundresses, draymen, pa-

perboys, woodcutters, and other service jobs. A few could be found in the professions as lawyers, nurses, auditors, and constables. Table 12 summarizes the occupational changes among Mexican-Americans who found employment in these new vocations. Since this table presents noncumulative entries into new jobs, it is a useful way of gauging changing opportunities.

During the 'fifties, over 100 individuals found new jobs, but this was only about 12 percent of the total work force. After 1860 there was a significant drop in the number of those who were able to enter new occupations: only 2 percent of the total Spanish-speaking work force participated in the growth of occupations in the city in the decade 1860–1870. The situation had improved somewhat by 1880, but still only about 6 percent of employed Mexican-Americans could be found in new jobs. It would appear, then, that up until 1860 there were some opportunities available, and that these were mostly in the skilled occupations. After this

TABLE 12

Mexican-Americans Employed in New Occupations, 1850–1880

Occupational Category[a]	1850	1860	1870	1880
Professional	1	9	2	9
Mercantile	19	11	2	5
Skilled	8	50	1	15
Manual	9	32	3	6
Total entries	37	102	8	35
Entries as a percentage of employed Mexican-Americans	10%	12%	2%	6%

SOURCE: Computer analysis of manuscript census returns.

a. A new occupation was defined as any occupation not listed in the Mexican census of 1844 for Los Angeles which later became a category of employment for Mexican-Americans.

date there was a rapid decline in all occupational opportunities.

If we compare the shifting new job openings available to skilled and manual laborers after 1860, the
skilled occupations offered more chances for employment than the unskilled callings. It may have been that
increased mechanization lowered the skills required of
workers, so that it became progressively easier to enter
certain occupations as the decades passed. Large-scale
Anglo-American immigration to Los Angeles, especially after the completion of the railroad in the mid-
1870's, also led to increased competition for new skilled
and manual jobs, resulting in the exclusion of many
Mexican-Americans from these trades by 1880.

Three decades of commercial growth in Los Angeles
affected the occupational structure of the Spanish-
speaking in a number of ways: (1) new jobs were
created, which resulted in the employment of Mexican-
Americans in skilled and unskilled occupations; (2)
the proportion of unskilled laborers in the community
remained high, but not quite as high as in the Mexican period; (3) several skilled Mexican-American
trades were eliminated by economic and technological
changes; (4) opportunities declined for rancheros and
merchants.

But the overall employment situation for La Raza
was ambiguous. The entrance of some Mexican-
Americans into new skilled vocations, and the slow
growth of a professional class, indicate a gradual improvement in the job situation for some. But the decline in opportunities among ranchers, farmers, shop-
keepers, and merchants probably cancelled out these
gains for La Raza as a whole. During the American era,
the Mexican-American occupational structure was
stagnant, with little opportunity for significant upward mobility. La Raza had an underdeveloped middle
class and a declining upper class. The working class—
the laborers and field hands—dominated Mexican-
American society.

On the whole, the traditional thesis of Mexican-

American decline following the war with the United States applies most pointedly to the Californio landowners. For the developing professional and skilled classes, American domination brought a slight increase in opportunities. For the mass of Mexican-American laborers, there was little change in socioeconomic mobility from the Mexican era. As the population and economy of Los Angeles grew under American domination, the Mexican-American population remained relatively stable. Thus La Raza played a decreasing role in the social, economic, and demographic growth of the city.

CHAPTER THREE

Changes in the Urban Family

In the decades following the Treaty of Guadalupe Hidalgo, the Mexican-American family absorbed the brunt of the economic and cultural shocks that marked the transition from national to ethnic status. The all-important activities of birth, child-rearing, schooling, marriage, work, and death acquired meaning primarily within the family unit. It was here that historical and economic forces were etched into the personalities of thousands of Spanish-speaking persons who, for however short a period of time, lived in the pueblo. Long a subject of sociological study and romantic stereotyping, the Mexican-American family and its historical evolution are still shrouded in mystery. Perhaps this is understandable in a people whose family life has for so long been intensely private, shaped by the forces of religion and tradition.[1]

New developments in the methodology of family historical studies have made it possible for researchers to go beyond tedious genealogical narrations or sub-

---

1. For those who would investigate Mexican-American family history, the only guide that exists is a brief sociological article by Robert Staples; but this pioneering work is an unsatisfactory model as a historical study. Robert Staples, "The Mexican-American Family: Its Modifications Over Time and Space," *Phylon*.

A number of sociological studies, now dated, may provide a source for historians of the Mexican-American family. All of these studies are for the twentieth century, however. Among these sources are: Kathleen Gonzales, "The Mexican Family in San Antonio" (Master's thesis); Sigurd Johnson, "Family Organization in Spanish-American Cultural Areas," *Sociol. and Soc. Res.;* Norman D. Humphrey, "The Changing Structure of the Detroit Mexican

jective accounts of daily life.[2] Although such research may serve as a guide for investigating the American family, there are special characteristics of the Mexican-American population's local history that pose questions not normally asked. Two themes that run through the present literature on the family are, first, the degree to which industrialization has changed the average family's size and composition and, second, the relation of the family to socioeconomic mobility. These themes can be analyzed using census data available for Mexican-American families in the nineteenth century. But another problem posed by the ethnic transformation of the Spanish-speaking population is the degree to which the Mexican family was influenced by Anglo-American culture. To what degree did the family become an agent of acculturation? Did La Raza find in the family a refuge where "traditional" values could be preserved, or did the family disintegrate under the pressures of cultural conflict? This chapter will explore these questions.

The Traditional Family

In the Mexican period, upper-class Californio marriages united the couple with an extended family, the Catholic Church, and the community. Weddings assumed the importance of public holidays, with elaborate rituals and endless feasting. The marriage of María

---

Family," *Am. Sociol. Rev.*; William Madsen, *The Mexican-Americans of South Texas*; Jolen Leonard and E. P. Loomis, *The Culture of a Contemporary Rural Community: El Cerrito, New Mexico*; Margaret Clark, *Health in the Mexican-American Culture*; Sister Mary John Murray, *A Socio-Cultural Study of 118 Mexican Families Living in a Low-Rent Housing Project in San Antonio, Texas.*

2. Richard Sennett, *Families Against the City: Middle Class Homes of Industrial Chicago, 1872–1890*; John Demos, *A Little Commonwealth: Family Life in Plymouth Colony*; Phillip J. Greven, *Four Generations: Population, Land and Family in Colonial Andover, Massachusetts*; Edmund Morgan, *The Puritan Family: Religion and Domestic Relations in Seventeenth-Century New England*; Kenneth Lockridge, *Literacy in Colonial New England: An Inquiry into the Social Context of Literacy in the Early Modern West.*

Teresa de la Guerra to William E. P. Hartnell in 1825 was typical. On Friday, the day before the wedding, the pueblo held a fiesta. In the early-morning hours of the next day, the bride and her father went to the church dressed in traditional black. About ten o'clock, after many hours of prayer, the groom arrived, and the wedding mass (*misa de boda*) began. It lasted two hours. Most of this time the couple knelt before the priest joined by a scarf symbolizing their union. After the mass, the bride's parents, showing a generosity commensurate with their wealth, distributed gifts to the crowd that had waited patiently outside. "Then from the Church steps a procession formed. Choir boys were followed by a garlanded *carreta* drawn by two white oxen in which rode the wedded pair. . . . There were dashing caballeros, and some Indians and humble people on foot. All together, it was a colorful and noisy cavalcade which made its way with the singing and music across the presidio to the comandante's house, where a noonday dinner awaited them."[3] After the wedding lunch (*comida de boda*), the pueblo celebrated in earnest with a fiesta that began at the bride's father's house and later moved to the plaza. This lasted for several days and nights with feasting and dancing until the entire community was exhausted.[4]

With variations, depending on the parent's wealth, this elaborate wedding celebration remained a central social event in the life of the Mexican-American family. Weddings were always community affairs and invitations were almost never required. After the formalities and fiestas, the parents, especially those of the bride, were expected to strictly supervise the lives of the new couple. Parents often retained the right to punish their married children, and they expected complete submission. The couple owed obedience to all the older fam-

3. Susanna Bryant Dakin, *The Lives of William Hartnell*, pp. 97–98.

4. For a description of similar wedding ceremonies, see Alfred Robinson, *Life in California*, pp. 133–147; and Dakin, *A Scotch Paisano*, pp. 168–169.

ily members, regardless of blood relationship.[5] Arnaz recalled that "the respect for their elders was great—paternal authority did not end with the death of the father—the same respect was due to the mother and with little difference to all the elder family members, whether or not they were parents."[6]

Arranged marriages were the rule rather than the exception. Couples usually continued to live in the bride's father's house. The son-in-law received an allowance for the support of his family while working for his father-in-law.[7] Of course, among the poorer classes, these economic and social relationships were less frequent. But still, even for them, a tone of traditional paternalism prevailed.

The social and economic upheavals that began with the American era gradually modified this traditional family structure in many ways. The most important change was that women increasingly became heads of households (see Table 13). In 1844, only 13 percent of all heads of families were women. Many of these were widows, and a few were probably women whose husbands were absent during the census. By 1880, more than 31 percent of Mexican-American families were headed by women. In less than 40 years, the female-centered family had become a significant institution in the Mexican-American community. A proportion of

5. "A son or daughter, although married, was under the orders of the parents; and even though their children were married, the parents had the right to punish them and the children had to suffer the punishment with humility." (ORIGINAL SPANISH: "Un hijo o hija, aunque casado o casada, estaba sometido a los ordenes de los padres; y aún en ese estado tenían estos el derecho de castigar a aquellos, y los hijos tenían que sufrir el castigo con humildad.") Antonio Coronel, *Cosas de California* (ms., Bancroft Library), p. 299.

6. ORIGINAL SPANISH: "El respeto a sus mayores era grande—la autoridad paterna no cesaba sino con la vida del padre—el mismo respeto se tenía a las madres, y con poco diferencia a los ancianos, aun cuando no fuesen parientes." José Arnaz, *Recuerdos* (ms., Bancroft Library), p. 24.

7. Coronel, p. 230.

TABLE 13
Spanish-Speaking Heads of Households,
1844–1880

Year	Male	Female	Total	Percentage of females to total
1844	201	30	231	13
1850	167	53	220	24
1860	329	127	456	28
1870	302	167	469	35
1880	323	146	469	31

SOURCE: Computer analysis of manuscript census returns.

the increase in female heads of households was probably due to census errors. Anglo census takers may have missed counting husbands who were temporarily absent. Temporary abandonment resulting from fewer local job opportunities may also have accounted for the increase. Given the strong religious sanctions against it, divorce was probably not a cause.

Another reason for the increasing numbers of women heading families may have been a higher death rate among men. A sample of 250 Mexican Americans who died during the period 1877–1887 shows that adult males had a higher mortality rate than adult females (Table 14).[8] The possibility that Mexican-

8. These samples were drawn from the Los Angeles City *Index to Deaths, 1877–1887* (L.A. County Recorder's Office). A detailed breakdown of the causes of death, grouped in seven categories and omitting infant mortalities, is as follows:

Cause of Death	Male	Female
1. Accidental	5	3
2. Nervous System	9	4
3. Respiratory	20	31
4. Infectious	70	52
5. Heart	3	1
6. Organic	5	3
7. Unspecified	21	17
Totals	133	111

TABLE 14
Death Rate Among a Sample of 250
Mexican-Americans in Los Angeles,
1877–1887

Age	Male	Female
22–30	16	11
31–40	17	10
41–50	11	11
51–60	7	4
Over 60	13	14

SOURCE: Los Angeles County Recorder's Office, *Index to Deaths, 1877–1887*, vol. 1 (ms.).

American men died at an earlier age than their women is supported by the large number of women who were listed as widows in the 1880 census. In most families without men, the women lived off the incomes of their children and relatives. Very few of them worked. In 1860, none were listed as having occupations, and in 1880 only 12 could be counted as employed heads of households.

Besides the increase in female heads of households, there were also a significant number of common-law marriages, unions which avoided the formalities of religious ceremony and circumvented the controls of the extended family.[9] Since the Mexican census-takers

---

See Richard Griswold del Castillo, "Health and the Mexican-Americans in Los Angeles, 1850–1887," *J. Mex.-Am. Hist.*

9. An extended family is a nuclear family with one or more relatives, through blood or marriage, living within the household. A nuclear family is defined as any household with a couple, male and female, living together with or without children; it also includes single parents with children. A single family is defined as one or more unmarried adults living together without children. For further discussion of the difficulties involved in family typology, along with a more complete definition of various types of families, see Peter Laslett and Richard Wall (eds.), *Household and Family in Past Time*, p. 31.

listed wives by their maiden names, there are no comparative statistics prior to 1850. There is some evidence that during the Mexican era unmarried couples were accepted by society.[10] In 1850, 7 percent of the couples in Los Angeles could be classified as common-law unions. Throughout the following decades this proportion remained about the same, despite increases in population.[11]

California did not recognize the legal responsibilities of common-law couples until 1862, when the civil code made free unions valid. Prior to this time, local traditions determined the duties of common-law couples.[12] Not until 1924 did the state pass laws to require that the husband financially support his common-law wife and children.[13]

10. "Habían otros . . . quienes tenían la reputación de vivir en concubinage, o de frestrase a los halagos de los hombres, y sin embargo eran admitidos el trato de los gentes." Arnaz, *Recuerdos,* p. 15.

11. Common-law marriages as a percentage of the married couples in Los Angeles, 1844–1880:

Year	Common-Law Unions
1844	No data, since the census listed wives by their maiden names
1850	7.7%
1860	7.5%
1870	5.1%
1880	7.3%

SOURCE: Computer analysis of manuscript census returns.

The constant proportion of unmarried couples in the pueblo suggests that economic and political changes did not radically affect this aspect of family life. The statistics on free-union marriages are subject to all the errors associated with using the census documents, in particular the Spanish convention of a married woman keeping her maiden name by adding it to her husband's surname. This custom, still practiced in Latin America, may have confused the Anglo census-takers, causing them to list the wrong last names for women. There is no proof that this actually happened, and many other couples were reported with the same last name, which indicates that this confusion, if it existed, was not universal.

12. Barbara A. Armstrong, *California Family Law,* vol. 1, p. 3.

13. *Ibid.,* p. 1095.

The Mexican family structure was also changed by legislation that undercut traditional community-property laws. Equal ownership of property between husband and wife had been one of the mainstays of the Spanish and Mexican family systems. Community-property laws were written into the civil codes with the intention of strengthening the economic controls of the wife and her relatives.[14] The American government incorporated these Mexican laws into the state constitution, but later court decisions interpreted these statutes so as to undermine the wife's economic rights. In 1861, the legislature passed a law that allowed the deceased wife's property to revert to her husband. Previously it had been inherited by her children and relatives if she died without a will.[15] In 1864, the children lost the right to inherit if their father died intestate. If he died leaving a will, only half of his patrimony was subject to testimentary disposition.[16] These new laws and court rulings strengthened the property rights of the husband at the expense of his wife and their children. When combined with the incidence of women serving as heads of households, this meant profound changes in the traditional family structure.

Relations Between the Sexes

Laws, traditions, and elaborate rituals created powerful sanctions to support the institution of marriage among the Spanish-speaking. In the American era, relationships between the sexes became more complex, due to increasing dislocation resulting from economic and demographic change. In the early years, the patriarchal extended family presided over the social life of Los Angeles—although, even then, relations between the sexes were characterized by a certain degree of frontier equality. This was especially so during the harvest. Ygnacio del Valle remembered that "men, women and

14. *Ibid.*, p. 431.   15. *Ibid.*, p. 586.   16. *Ibid.*, p. 587.

children all labored during the harvest," and this same
kind of social equality could be observed during the
rodeos, when women worked alongside men preparing
hides for market.[17]

As Los Angeles ceased to be a small rural town, this
frontier equality gave way to more structured roles.
The growth of prostitution among non-Indians was
one indication that traditional relationships were break-
ing down. In 1836 the census listed 15 non-Indian
women of the pueblo as "mala vida," or prostitutes.
There had been prostitution before this, but it had been
largely confined to the Yang-na Indian village. During
the Gold Rush, many Anglo women came to Los
Angeles for this purpose; later, Chinese and Black
women added a cosmopolitan flavor. Prostitution was
legal until 1909; the "respectable families" tolerated it
because, by an 1874 law, houses of prostitution were
confined to the barrio.[18] That prostitution was limited
to Sonora Town did not necessarily mean that it served
only the needs of the Mexican-American community.
In many respects, old Los Angeles resembled a present-day border town—vices forbidden in the Anglo
community could be satisfied in the barrio.

The Mexican-Americans of Los Angeles romanticized their feelings about men and women in songs,
poems, and plays. Traditionally, the serenade was the
medium through which a young man expressed his
love for his girlfriend. The popularity of this poetic
form and peripatetic tradition continued into the American era. As late as 1883, mariachi bands continued to
hire themselves out to accompany suitors. Luckily,
some of the original lyrics of the singers have survived
to this day.

17. "Men, women, and children all worked during the
harvest—all worked with their hands—each worker carried on his
back a basket into which the grain was thrown." Translation of
Pío Pico, *Narración Historica* (ms., Bancroft Library).
18. William W. Robinson, *Tarnished Angels: Paradisical Turpitude
in Los Angeles Revealed,* pp. 14–15.

La Serenade

If there is an enchanting being in the world,
It is you alone, my beautiful.
And as an angel in heaven surpasses all,
So too do you.

And the man in his sorrow discovers
An object of joy and consolation.
It is you whom God in Heaven
Sent to earth for my welfare.

Come to the window, angelic woman,
Light brighter than the star Prey.
Pure Virgin of light that you are, my beloved,
You are my happiness, my love, and my law.[19]

With variations, serenades such as this followed a similar rhetorical development. They praised the beloved, comparing her to divine beings and implying that she had mysterious powers over her lover. Often there was some acknowledgment of suffering, and the serenade ended with a plea for the girl to come to her window.

19. ORIGINAL SPANISH:

La Seranate

Si hay un ser hechicero en el mundo
Ese ser eres tu sola bella
Y si un angel del cielo descuella sobre todo tu
    eres también.

Y si encuentra en su pena el hombre
Un objeto de dicha y consuelo.
Eres tu que el Señor desde el cielo
A la tierra te envió por mi bien.

A la ventana mujer angélica sol más galona que
    astre prey.
Sol Vírgen pura que tú eres mi querer
Tú, mi ventura, mi amor, mi ley.

"La Seranate," 1877 (ms., Coronel Collection, L.A. County Mus. Nat. Hist.). The English translation of this and subsequent poems follows the general principles suggested by Jacques Barzun and Henry F. Graff in *The Modern Researcher: A Classic Manual on All Aspects of Research and Writing,* ch. 14.

Mexican-American love songs and poems tended to emphasize suffering. "La Mujer," a song analyzing female psychology, ended with the stanza:

> Poor woman, you hold back a flood of tears,
> And sorrow dries your heart.
> The hand of pain marks your face.
> Poor woman, born to tears.[20]

An excerpt from a poem by Francisco P. Ramirez, "A Mi María Antonia," illustrated the same theme:

> I don't know—but thought
> Tells me that we are both suffering,
> And that in the same torment
> Our souls are consumed.[21]

It could be that the painful sentiments expressed in love poems and songs reflected the poetic conventions of the period, and that the day-to-day relations between the sexes were characterized by a more prosaic male dominance. Mexican-American women had their traditional place, in the home. It became a matter of public concern when, in 1856, girls began to be admitted to public schools. Francisco P. Ramirez, editor of *El Clamor Público,* argued that the community should accept this change because women were too unstable and emotional anyway, and that "una educación cultivada" would discipline them and make them more rational.[22]

---

20. ORIGINAL SPANISH:

> Pobre mujer su vestro llanto querro
> Y seco el corazón la pena siente.
> La Mano de dolor marca su frente.
> Pobre mujer nació para llorar.

"La Mujer," 1877 (ms., Coronel Collection, L.A. County Mus. Nat. Hist.).

21. ORIGINAL SPANISH:

> No sé—pero el pensamiento me dice que ambos sufrimos,
> Y que en un mismo tormento nuestras almas consumimos.

Francisco P. Ramirez, "A Mi María Antonio," *El Grito.*

22. *El Clamor Público,* April 26, 1856, p. 2.

Antonio Coronel, in one of his philosophical moods, penned a small essay expressing his views: "The first woman [Eve] did not have any rivals; nevertheless, she wanted to obtain the apple; and since then, in a spirit of imitation, women have not ceased to accuse one another of this desire. . . . Man, born before woman, is therefore nobler than she."[23]

The assumption that women were more emotional and less noble than men, and should remain at home, must have been at odds with the growing reality of increased female involvement outside the family. A growing number of women were managing their own economic affairs, and a noticeable number were escaping the controls of their families by entering into common-law marriages. In more prosperous days, during the 'fifties and early 'sixties, many women worked; they composed 6 percent of the work force by 1860. Some of these working women supplemented their husbands' incomes. In the 1870's the number of working women declined, probably due to the depression. By 1880, working women reemerged to compose 13 percent of the Mexican-American work force. A significant change from earlier years was that most of these women worked as live-in servants (see Table 15).

Women also became prominent in the social life of the community, mainly in the theater as actresses and impresarios. In 1872, Señora Adelina Dominguez was the star of El Teatro Alcaron, and in the 'eighties and 'nineties Señora Laura Molla played a prominent role in organizing El Club Dramático Español which met in Hazard Pavilion. She also served as leading lady in many of its productions.[24] Women also became important in the traditional Mexican Independence Day

23. ORIGINAL SPANISH: "La mujer del Paraiso no tiene rivales; sin embargo quisó obtener la manzana y desde entonces, por espiritu de imitacion, los mujeres no han dejado de imputarla entre ellas. . . . El hombre que ha nacido antes que la mujer es de consiguiente más noble que ella." "La Mujer," 1877.

24. El Aguacero, March 31, 1878; Las Dos Repúblicas, Aug. 23, 1892; La Crónica, May 26, 1883.

TABLE 15
Mexican-American Women Working Outside the Home,
1850–1880

Year	Total Mexican-American work force	Women working Number	Percentage
1850	224	1	.4%
1860	614	39	6.0
1870	444	1	.2
1880	553	74	13.3

SOURCE: Manuscript census returns.

celebrations. They appeared in public to deliver poems and songs that complemented the lengthy speeches.[25] These were some indications that man-woman relations were beginning to evolve outside the traditional family. In spite of this, the vast majority of women continued to live lives circumscribed by their families and their men.

Marriage and Intermarriage

Prior to 1848, most of the foreigners who settled in the Los Angeles district married local women and became members of the Californio elite. Intermarriage with the daughters of the *gente de razón* was one route to upward mobility and social acceptance. The Californios, for their part, were not opposed to these alliances. During the American era, however, intermarriage took on a different meaning. Most of the Anglo immigrants who came during the Gold Rush were not at all interested in adapting to the local culture. In fact, many of them were violently opposed to things Mexican. Over the decades, increasing numbers of native-born daughters married these Anglo arrivals. During the 1850's, only about one marriage in ten was of this

25. *Las Dos Repúblicas,* Sept. 16, 1893, and Sept. 15, 1897.

mixed type; but after the depression of the 1860's, one marriage in three was mixed.

Although a few Mexican-American men married Anglo women, the vast majority of mixed marriages were between Anglo men and Mexican-American women.[26] As Table 16 shows, the rate of intermarriage increased, especially after 1864. This finding conflicts with the views of several historians who have assumed that intermarriages were more common in the 1850's. Both Carey McWilliams and Leonard Pitt have concluded that mixed marriages declined after 1850, due to worsening racial relations in the pueblo.[27]

It may have been true that in prosperous years the upper-class Californios tended to intermarry less frequently. But the depressed economic situation after 1860 seems to have encouraged many Mexican-Americans to intermarry, perhaps in hopes of improving their status. Weakening of traditional family ties also gave women more freedom to select their marriage partners. Another consideration must be the numerical increase in the Anglo male population. After 1860, there were in California—and in Los Angeles in particular—a great many more men than women. And the majority of these men were Anglo Americans.[28] By 1880, there were still 5 men for every 4 women in the pueblo. The lure of intermarriage must have been even greater for Spanish-speaking women, since Anglo men were in control of the political and economic life of the city.

26. In 1867 Pedro Vadillo married Angelina Courney and Barnabe Machado married Mary Murphy. In 1870 Pedro Vejar married Mary E. Gross, and in 1874 Manuel Rubio married Concepción Warner. In most of these cases, the Mexican-American men were in the upper economic class.

27. McWilliams, *North from Mexico*, p. 91; Pitt, "Submergence of the Mexican in California, 1846–1890" (Ph.D. diss.), p. 310.

28. Warren Thompson estimated that Los Angeles' sex ratio (the proportion of men to 100 women) was 132 in 1850, 155 in 1860, 137 in 1870, and 124 in 1880. See Warren S. Thompson, *Growth and Change in California's Population*, p. 48.

TABLE 16
Intermarriage,
1856–1875

Year	Total number of Mexican-Americans married (1)	Total number of marriages with Anglos (2)	Percentage of mixed marriages (2/1)
1856	15	2	13.4%
1857	25	2	8.0
1858	41	6	14.8
1859	34	3	8.9
1860	21	4	19.0
1861	0	1	100.0
1862	17	4	23.5
1863	25	3	12.0
1864	30	11	45.9
1865	20	2	10.0
1866	24	11	45.9
1867	20	8	40.0
1868	17	8	47.0
1869	25	10	40.0
1870	25	16	64.0
1871	11	4	36.4
1872	12	4	33.3
1873	10	5	50.5
1874	25	6	24.0
1875	35	4	11.2

SOURCE: Los Angeles County Recorder's Office, *Index to Marriage Certificates, 1851–1876*, vol. 1 (ms.).

The *Index to Marriage Certificates*, rather than the marriage documents of Our Lady Queen of Angels parish church, has been selected to study Mexican-American marriage patterns. By law, all marriages were registered with the county officials, and so this source is more complete. In later years more and more Mexican-Americans tended to be married by Justices of the Peace and even by Protestant clergymen.

Women married young in Mexican California; 15 was not considered too tender an age for an arranged marriage. While it is hard to obtain unequivocal data on this subject, it appears that the custom of early marriage declined. Over the years, the proportion of older married women increased, suggesting that fewer and fewer young women were getting married. In 1844, for example, more than 50 percent of the married women were between 17 and 30 years of age. The percentage of married women 17 and younger declined from 2 percent in 1860 to 0.6 percent in 1880 (see Table 17).

Changes in the age structure of the population may explain why women tended to marry later in 1880 than they did in 1844. Prior to 1860, Mexican-American men outnumbered women in the most fertile age groups (ages 15–40). Only in 1870 did the sex ratio begin to reverse. As the supply of women became more plentiful, early marriages declined. Diminishing family controls and economic depression may also have contributed to the decline of early marriages.

The Family and Fertility

Some literature exists on the late-nineteenth-century Anglo family and its child-rearing practices, but almost nothing is available on the Mexican-American family during the same period. Faced with the difficulty of obtaining primary source material after 1848, the researcher's only recourse is to marriage records, birth certificates, baptismal documents, and school lists. From these it is possible to partly reconstruct the fate of children within the Spanish-speaking family.[29]

29. Herbert Howe Bancroft's vast collection of California documents is most useful when researching the period prior to 1850. All of the reminiscences he collected from the Mexican residents of Los Angeles during the period 1877–78 were taken with the purpose of documenting the Mexican, not the American, era. A few of those whom Thomas Savage interviewed did make parenthetical remarks on contemporary life, but the bulk of their reminiscences were of the years prior to the Mexican War. Other collections such as the Del Valle Collection and the Coronel Collec-

TABLE 17

Age Distribution of Married Mexican-American Women

Age	1844		1850		1860		1870		1880	
1–17	2	1%	0	0%	3	1%	2	1%	2	.6%
18–21	17	9	15	10	33	12	20	7	21	7
22–30	79	45	67	48	115	41	122	44	111	37
31–40	48	27	41	29	74	27	78	28	107	35
41–50	17	10	12	8	36	13	33	12	36	12
over 50	10	8	4	5	13	6	17	8	23	8
Totals	173	100%	139	100%	274	100%	272	100%	300	99.4%

SOURCE: Manuscript census returns.

The baptismal records of the Church Nuestra Señora La Reina de Los Angeles are available, and are the best single source for studying the birthrate. Because of strong religious traditions, most Spanish-speaking parents baptized their children. The plaza church was the only one available to city residents prior to 1879. The majority of the parish was Spanish-surnamed, although there were also some Italian, French, and Irish parishioners. From this source we can estimate the probable birthrate for a large sample of the Mexican-American population (see Table 18).

As can be seen, the birthrate declined very rapidly after 1850. During the entire nineteenth century, the nationwide birthrate fell by only 14 percent. But in the 40 years after 1850, the Mexican-American birthrate fell by more than 56 percent.[30]

The decennial data on women of child-bearing age ignores the annual birthrate trends. The accompanying chart is a graphic representation of the year-by-year fluctuations in baptisms from 1844 to 1873. Generally the number of baptisms increased from 1853 to 1863, then declined by more than half thereafter. By 1873, the last date for which there is readily available documentation, the number of baptisms about equaled those of the Mexican era, despite the increase in population.

One would expect to find an increasing birthrate during the early 1850's, since Mexican-Americans enjoyed a degree of prosperity then. But there are other possible explanations for this increase. Edward A.

---

tion, both at the Los Angeles County Museum of Natural History, have bits and pieces dealing with family life. But here, as with the Bancroft documents, the majority are drawn from the Mexican period. Material dating after 1850 is mostly about political and economic affairs. A few of the more useful of the reminiscences, for reconstructing family life after the conquest, are: José Matías Moreno, *Documentos para la historia de California,* 1878; Antonio Coronel, *Cosas de California;* 1877; Ramon Sepúlveda, *Dictación,* 1888; and Vicente Lugo, *Dictación,* 1888. All are located in the Bancroft Library.

30. Social Science Research Council (eds.), *The Statistical History of the United States from Colonial Times to the Present,* p. 23.

TABLE 18
Birthrate for City and County Mexican-Americans,
1850–1870

Year	Number of children baptized	Number of women of child-bearing age[a]	Birthrate[b]
1850	107	313	341
1855	164	474	345
1860	93	633	146
1865	106	546	194
1870	69	459	150

SOURCE: Genealogical Records Committee of California, State Society of the Daughters of the American Revolution, *Libro de bautismos de N.S. de Los Angeles en la ciudad de Los Angeles,* libros I–IV (m.s.), University of California, Los Angeles, Special Collections.

a. Defined as women between 15 and 40 years of age. Statistics for 1855 and 1865 are interpolated from the decennial census.

b. Children baptized per 1,000 women of child-bearing age.

Wrigley concludes that, in some areas of the world, modernization has had the effect, at least initially, of increasing the birthrate.[31] He believes that this was caused by a combination of factors: an imbalance in the sex ratio (more men than women), a high infant mortality rate, new suckling habits, and a rise in the fertile age group's life expectancy. All of these factors may have operated to increase the number of births of Mexican-Americans in Los Angeles. We have no data for Mexican-American infant mortality prior to 1877, but after this date it was very high. Almost 40 percent of the total number of Mexican-American deaths in the period 1877–78 were of children under 5 years of age. The Anglo-American infant mortality rate during the same period was 17 percent.[32]

31. Edward A. Wrigley, *Population and History*.
32. Griswold del Castillo, "Health," pp. 19–22.

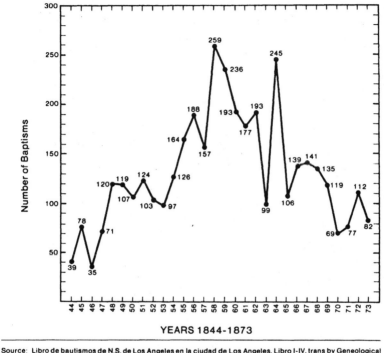

Source: Libro de bautismos de N.S. de Los Angeles en la ciudad de Los Angeles, Libro I-IV, trans by Geneological Records Committee of California, State Society of the Daughters of the American Revolution, 1945, Department of Special Collections, University of California, Los Angeles.

7. Baptisms in Los Angeles 1844–1873. Taken from *Libro de baustismos de N.S. de Los Angeles en la ciudad de Los Angeles,* Libro I–IV, trans. by Genealogical Records Committee of California, State Society of the Daughters of the American Revolution, 1945, Department of Special Collections, University of California, Los Angeles.

8. Young Mexicanos on an early baseball team. Left to right: Samovar Arguello, Jesús Pacheco (4th from left), José Arguello (7th from left), Miguel Aguirre (10th from left), Carlos P. de la Guerra (13th from left), José Mascarel. Reginaldo del Valle, a future state senator, is the boy with the bat on his shoulders. Courtesy of the Huntington Library.

It would be wrong to interpret these limited statistics on births and deaths as indicative of long-range population trends for the Mexican-Americans of Los Angeles. Although the birthrate was on the decline after 1864, we cannot infer that it continued to fall in later decades.[33] However, a decline in the ratio of men to women would seem to indicate that the prospects for increasing fertility were unlikely. But this trend could have been offset through continued immigration or by an improvement in life expectancy.

What of the declining number of births (baptisms) after 1864? Demographers have noted that the birthrate in industrializing countries, after an initial increase, has fallen at a steady rate. Families have been motivated to limit the number of children in expectation of a better standard of living.[34] It can be inferred, however, that these optimistic considerations do not take into account the effect of racial discrimination and economic disenfranchisement—realities for Mexican-American Angelenos after 1848.

After the Mexican War, Spanish-speaking families tended to be smaller: the average number of children fell from 3 to 2.5 per family.[35] It was due to the combined influences of immigration and religion that family size did not decline more rapidly. The Roman

33. Conceivably it would be possible to measure Mexican-American births using the city's Register of Births which began in 1879. This would involve analyzing over 200,000 handwritten birth certificates arranged alphabetically, not chronologically. Such an analysis is beyond the limits of this study. For a discussion of the many complexities and problems involved in such a labor, see Phillip M. Hauser and Otis Dudley Duncan (eds.), *The Study of Population: An Inventory and Appraisal*, pp. 409–414.

34. Wrigley, *Population and History*, p. 191.

35. The average number of children per family was as follows:

Year	Average No. Children
1844	2.9%
1850	3.0%
1860	2.4%
1870	2.4%
1880	2.5%

Catholic strictures against birth control did not contribute to the decline of the Mexican-American family, but economic considerations diluted the Church's influence. Historically, family limitation has been more widespread among members of the upper classes.[36] Some of the wealthier Mexican-Americans did tend to have fewer children, but this was not a noticeable trend until after 1870. In general, the wealthy and the poor alike raised about the same number of children. Family size bore no significant relationship to the place of birth of the parents. Neither was it related to the parents' education—the more educated and literate parents tended to have as many children as less educated couples. All this seems to confirm the view that the historical conditions of economic depression and discrimination influenced the decline in family size for all Mexican-Americans, irrespective of their socioeconomic status, nativity, or education.

The Family and Education

One of the most significant developments affecting the Mexican-American family after 1850 was the increased numbers of children who regularly attended public schools. During the Mexican period, the pobladores had to rely on the sporadic efforts of ex-soldiers whom the *ayuntamiento* periodically appointed as schoolmasters.[37] Needless to say, the soldier-teachers'

36. A comparison of property holdings with the number of children in the family shows no correlation prior to 1870. T. Lynn Smith has found that socioeconomic class and fertility may be positively related in contemporary Latin American countries, where the upper classes tend to have even larger families than the lower classes. This was not the case for the Mexican-American upper class in the late nineteenth century. See T. Lynn Smith, "Current Population Trends in Latin America," *Am. J. Sociol.*

37. A good survey of the Mexican schools can be found in C. Toto, Jr., "A History of Education in California, 1800–1850" (Ph.D. diss.). Other works useful for understanding education during the Mexican regime are: James M. Guinn, *A History of California and an Extended History of Los Angeles and Environs,* vol. 1, pp. 12–13, and "Old-Time Schools and School Masters of Los

discipline was strict. Corporal punishments were frequent, and attendance was limited to boys. The Mexican pueblo school never attained the importance of an established institution, since the ayuntamiento lacked funds, trained teachers, and political stability. As a consequence, the citizens developed the idea that the Church and family should be responsible for moral and intellectual training. The Church's role was limited to sporadic catechism classes and sermons. Some rancheros and wealthy town dwellers ran informal schools for their children and for those of their relatives. A few sent their children to Mexico City for a more formal education.[38] From 1848 to 1853 the Common Council, which replaced the ayuntamiento, employed Francisco Bustamente and Ygnacio Coronel to teach a Spanish-language school.[39]

In 1853 the Council finally set up an English-language public school system, and in the next year built the first schoolhouse on the northwest corner of Spring and Second Streets.[40] By 1855 there were over 150 students attending this school, taught by three Anglo teachers. Despite the fact that instruction was in English, relatively large numbers of Spanish-speaking students attended. By 1860, almost half of the students were Spanish-surnamed (see Table 19). In later years, however, the proportion of Mexican-Americans in the

Angeles," *Annual Hist. Soc. So. Calif.*; Bancroft, *History of California*, vol. 4, p. 403; Newmark and Newmark (eds.), *Sixty Years in Southern California, 1853–1913*, p. 105; Charles D. Willard, *Herald's History of Los Angeles City*, p. 105; Lugo, "Vida de un Ranchero," *Q. Hist. Soc. So. Calif.*; Thompson, West, and Wilson (eds.), *History of Los Angeles County, California*, p. 73; and Susan M. Dorsey, "History of Schools and Education in Los Angeles" (ms., L.A. Public Library).

38. Arnaz, *Recuerdos*, p. 25. Angustias de la Guerra's two brothers, Pablo and Francisco, were sent to the Mexican capital for their education. See Ord, *Occurrences in Hispanic California*, p. 13; Guinn, *History of California*, p. 381.

39. James M. Guinn, "Pioneer School Superintendents," *Q. Hist. Soc. So. Calif.*

40. Guinn, *History of California*, p. 16.

TABLE 19
School Attendance of Los Angeles Children, 1860–1880

	1860	1870	1880
Total number attending school[a]	245	904	2,139
Total number of Mexican-Americans attending school[b]	118	105	136
Total number of Anglo-Americans attending school	127	700	2,003
Number of school-age Mexican-Americans	415	421	358
Number of school-age Anglo-Americans[c]	n.d.	1,983	3,175
Percentage of school-age Mexican-Americans attending school	43%	25%	38%
Percentage of school-age Anglo-Americans attending school	n.d.	40%	63%

n.d. = no data available.

a. Los Angeles County Board of Education, *Annual Report, 1883–1884*, p. 70; statistics for 1860 are interpolated from James M. Guinn, *A History of California and an Extended History of Los Angeles and Environs*, vol. 1, p. 384. Age categories are for ages 5–17.

b. SOURCE: Manuscript census returns. Age categories are for ages 5–19.

c. Age categories are for ages 5–19.

public schools became smaller. By 1880, only about 6 percent of all those attending schools were Mexican-Americans, even though in that year Spanish-speaking children made up 15 percent of the school-age population. Nevertheless, Mexican-American school attendance was comparable to that of the Anglo-Americans. In every census year for which there are data, between 25 and 40 percent of Mexican-American children attended school. This compares favorably with the attendance records of Anglo children, 40 percent of whom were in school in 1870. Truancy was a problem for both groups, since attendance was not mandatory until the 1890's. Many families needed the additional income that could be earned by their school-age children. School officials recognized that economic necessity, not negligence, was a major reason for the low attendance of both groups. Another factor affecting the school attendance of Spanish-speaking children was the Californio prejudice against schooling girls. Few girls attended the public schools in the early years.

That a relatively large proportion of Mexican-American children continued to attend school demonstrated a persistent hope on the part of their parents in the face of considerable difficulties. Not only the language but the curriculum was foreign to most Spanish-speaking students. Of course the public schools did not teach the traditional subjects of *La Doctrina Católica*. Instead they emphasized secular subjects. In the third grade, for example, children learned to use dictionaries, to compute decimal arithmetic, and to sightread music. By the time a child had completed the fourth grade, he had learned the fundamentals of English grammar, bookkeeping, biology, human physiology, and United States history.[41]

After 1870, Mexican-American school attendance was low. It may have been due to the hostility of parents who resented the punishments, both corporal and

41. Los Angeles Board of Education, *Annual Reports, 1883–1884,* pp. 68–69.

psychological, that Anglo teachers administered for speaking Spanish in the classroom. In 1883, for example, one parent assaulted an Anglo schoolteacher because he had beaten his daughter in the classroom.[42] Francisco P. Ramirez, writing in *El Clamor Público,* observed that "many parents do not send their children to the public school because there they teach only in English."[43] Pressure against the speaking of Spanish probably became more intense as Mexican-Americans gradually became a smaller minority of the pueblo's population.

Mexican-American parents responded to the lack of education in their native language in more positive ways, mainly by supporting bilingual schools, both parochial and secular. Until 1854 Ygnacio Coronel taught school in his house, charging 15 dollars a month per student.[44] In 1856 José R. Nielson, an Anglo linguist, began "un escuela para los niños de la raza Española" in Cristobal Aguilar's home near the plaza. He called the school La Mexicanita, and Nielson taught in both English and Spanish. That same year Don Luis Vignes, a Frenchman, organized a parochial school called La Escuela Católica, located adjacent to the offices of *El Clamor Público.* Vignes charged two pesos per month. La Escuela was open to both sexes, and instruction was in Spanish. Later, Vignes changed the name of the school to El Instituto Patriótico, in order to attract students with more secular interests.[45]

Many other organized efforts to establish a Spanish-language school failed due to the indifference of Anglo-American political leaders. In 1854 Don Antonio Coronel was a member of the school board and supported bilingual schooling. But his motions to institute Spanish-language instruction were vetoed by the

42. *La Crónica,* May 26, 1883.
43. *El Clamor Público,* Nov. 1, 1856.
44. Guinn, *History of California,* p. 382; Newmark and Newmark, *Sixty Years,* pp. 102–105.
45. *El Clamor Público,* Sept. 27, 1856; March 8, 1856.

other two school-board members, who were Anglos.[46] At least three times—in 1855, 1857, and 1858—parents petitioned the Common Council for funds to establish a bilingual school. The Council voted down these petitions.[47]

After 1858, most of the efforts to establish a Spanish-language school were pioneered by the Catholic Church. In 1861 the Sisters of Charity, most of whom were Spanish nuns, organized a bilingual parochial school called La Escuela de la Concepción Imaculada. Early in 1870, Spanish-speaking Catholic parishioners helped build St. Vincent's College, the first bilingual secondary school in the state. Examinations were in both languages, and many prominent Mexican-American families enrolled their children. In 1870 Reginaldo del Valle, who later became a prominent lawyer and statesman, gave the valedictory address of the graduating class.[48]

Contrary to what might be expected, the majority of those attending public and private schools during this period did not come from the wealthier families. The ranching and farming families were even less likely to have their children attend school than were those of the laboring classes. The statistics on attendance show that there was no significant correlation between schooling and the socioeconomic status of the family.[49]

46. After Coronel and for the next 120 years, only two other Mexican-Americans were appointed to the Los Angeles School Board: David J. Yorba and Pablo Dominguez, both in 1884. "School Board Reports, Bonds, etc." (Box 573, L.A. County Mus. Nat. Hist.).

47. Pitt, *Decline of the Californios*, p. 315; *El Clamor Público*, Nov. 1, 1856.

48. *La Crónica*, June 15, 1872.

49. Correlations of wealth (property and money) with numbers of children in school per family:

Year	Property with School Attendance	Personal Property School Attendance
1860	−.0093	−.0227
1870	.0074	.0143

The Family and Literacy

Researchers have found that increased literacy has been related to school attendance in nineteenth-century cities.[50] But this association was not evident among Mexican-Americans in Los Angeles. That those who attended schools did not become more literate is an indication that the public schools were failing to educate Mexican-American children in either Spanish or English. But the transiency of much of the Spanish-speaking population also worked against their receiving an adequate education.

Generally, Mexican-born heads of families tended to be more literate than the California-born. This was probably because most of the Mexican-born residents had been educated in their mother country. Psychologically, the immigrants and their children were more motivated to learn to read and write than were their conquered brothers. The Mexican immigrant, after all, had chosen to come to the United States in the hope of improving his life. California-born Mexican-Americans had had the foreign culture imposed upon them.

The difference in literacy between the Mexican- and California-born was especially pronounced in the 1850's and 1860's. Later the native-born began to improve; by 1880 they were at about the same level as the Mexican-born. For both groups, literacy was more prevalent than in earlier years. But still, fewer than one-quarter of the adult Mexican-American population could read and write. In comparison, almost 85 percent of the state population in 1880 was literate (see Table 20).[51]

50. Harvey Graff, studying Hamilton, Ontario (Canada), found that literacy was associated with school attendance, as did Stephen Thernstrom in his social history of Newburyport, Massachusetts. Harvey J. Graff, "Notes on Methods for Studying Literacy from the Manuscript Census," *Hist. Meth. Newsletter,* p. 14. Stephen Thernstrom, *Poverty and Progress,* pp. 145–146, 155–175.

51. U.S. Dept. of the Interior, Bureau of the Census, *Compendium of the Tenth Census (June 1, 1880),* Part 2, p. 1645. Out of a population (over 10 years old) of 681,062, the number listed as being able to read or write was 579,049.

TABLE 20

Literacy Related to Place of Birth

Year	Mexican-born			California-born		
	Number literate	Number of adults	Percentage literate	Number literate	Number of adults	Percentage literate
1850	43	180	24%	38	344	11%
1860[a]	114	546	21	74	667	11
1870	97	462	21	71	426	17
1880[b]	89	388	23	133	585	23

SOURCE: Manuscript census returns.

a. The 1850 and 1860 censuses counted those over 20 who could not read or write.
b. The 1870 and 1880 censuses counted those over 6 who could not read or write. In order to be consistent with prior censuses, I have selected those over 20 years of age who fit into this category.

Family organization also influenced the distribution of literacy. Children of extended families displayed a higher rate of literacy than did those who came from nuclear families. Extended families, defined as those with at least one relative living in the household of the nuclear family, were more able to teach their children how to read and write within the home, since the adult relatives often acted as teachers. In every census year, extended families had a higher rate of literacy than did nuclear families (see Table 21).

Literacy was also related to the socioeconomic class of parents. The extended families of those with professional, mercantile, and skilled occupations tended to be more literate than unskilled families. Regardless of whether or not he came from an extended family, the unskilled laborer was usually illiterate. In contrast to this, the upper occupational groups continued to exhibit a high degree of literacy. The ability to read and write was also positively related to property ownership. Those who owned over 500 dollars' worth of real and personal property had a higher literacy rate than those who owned less (see Tables 22 and 23). In this, the data on the Mexican-Americans of Los Angeles parallel those of other cities.[52]

The Family and Socioeconomic Mobility

There seem to be two views of the relationship between the family and economic mobility. One view sees the rise of the nuclear family as the dominant form, because it has better prepared its members for the rigors of industrial competition. Talcott Parsons, a leading proponent of this thesis, believes that the nuclear family has liberated individuals from the strict controls of the extended family. Others have argued that a high fertility rate, characteristic of the extended family, impedes the social and economic mobility of its members, since resources are used to rear children.[53]

52. Graff, "Notes on Methods," p. 14.
53. Richard Sennett, "Middle-Class Families and Urban Violence: The Experiences of the Chicago Community," in Stephen

TABLE 21
Literacy of Heads of Household by Type of Family

Type of Family:	1850		1860		1870		1880	
	Nuclear	Extended	Nuclear	Extended	Nuclear	Extended	Nuclear	Extended
Number of families	47	153	144	261	178	248	159	260
Number literate	11	60	70	156	91	155	90	157
Percentage literate	23.4	41.9	48.6	59.7	51.1	62.5	56.6	60.3
Thirty-year average percentage literate							44.9	56.1

SOURCE: Computer analysis of manuscript census returns.

TABLE 22
Literacy of Heads of Household by Occupational Status

Occupational status: Family type:	Ranchero		Professional		Mercantile		Skilled		Unskilled	
	Extended	Nuclear	Extended	Nuclear	Extended	Nuclear	Extended	Nuclear	Extended	Nuclear
Year										
1850 N=220	42%	16%	100%	100%	100%	100%	70%	42%	18%	10%
1860 N=530	82	93	100	0	88	95	80	68	34	30
1870 N=545	44	90	100	0	100	85	100	75	63	45
1880 N=521	71	88	100	66	95	90	72	57	45	48

SOURCE: Computer analysis of manuscript census returns.

N=Number of literate heads of households

TABLE 23
Literacy of Heads of Household by Categories of Wealth

			Income Level							
	$1–100		$101–500		$501–1000		$1001–5000		Over $5000	
Family type:	Extended	Nuclear	Extended	Nuclear	Extended	Nuclear	Extended	Nuclear	Extended	Nuclear
1850 N=220	7%	2%	21%	31%	8%	2%	25%	10%	8%	8%
1860 N=530	18	28	15	18	8	7	11	7	11	3
1870 N=545	2	1	13	11	5	2	15	10	6	1

SOURCE: Computer analysis of manuscript census returns.
Percentages do not add up to 100 since non-property-owning families have been omitted.

While the thesis that small families have advantages over larger ones in the competitive struggle would seem self-evident, several historians have challenged this argument in recent years. Phillippe Ariès, in a sweeping account of 300 years of family history, finds that the nuclear family, far from liberating the individual, has created formidable obstacles to economic advancement. In his view, the intensiveness of nuclear family life has overprotected and thus ill-prepared its members for participation in industrial life.[54]

Richard Sennett, in his book *Families Against the City*, has developed this idea even farther.[55] Studying middle-class Chicago families, he found that the nuclear structure was overdefensive and detrimental to upward mobility. With an impressive array of statistical data, he demonstrated that family life limited the experiences of its members by turning their energies inward rather than encouraging them to join the outside world. He discovered that extended families were more upwardly mobile because they were more work-oriented, less defensive and, in general, better trained for urban survival.[56]

Thernstrom and Richard Sennett (eds.), *Nineteenth-Century Cities: Essays in the New Urban History*, p. 409; United Nations, Population Division, *The Determinates and Consequences of Population Trends*, p. 79; Peter Blau and Otis Duncan, *The American Occupational Structure*, p. 367. A sample of authors who support the Parsons thesis includes: Morris Janowitz, "Some Consequences of Social Mobility in the United States," *Trans. Third World Congress Sociol.*; Peter M. Blau, "Social Mobility and Interpersonal Relations," *Am. Sociol. Rev.*; Pitirim Sorokin, *Social Mobility*, pp. 522–525; Marcel Breshard, "Mobilité Sociale et Dimension de la Famille," *Population*; Jerzy Berent, "Fertility and Social Mobility," *Population Studies*.

54. Although Ariès does not speak to the problem of socio-economic mobility per se, he does analyze the decline of what he calls sociability within the nuclear family. He believes that the nuclear family ceased to be integrated with the larger world and became more self-contained. See Phillippe Ariès, *Centuries of Childhood*, p. 407.

55. Sennett, *Families Against the City*.

56. *Ibid.*, pp. 188–217, 233. Sennett has been criticized for failing

Both Parsons and Ariès agree that the nuclear family is the dominant form of family organization in modern industrial society, but both have tended to view nuclear and extended families as absolute types. In recent years, sociologists have discovered another kind of family which they call the "modified extended." The modified extended family consists of a nuclear family plus relatives and friends who do not live in the household but who, nonetheless, act as helpers. Research indicates that the modified extended family is the most common type in industrial settings and is responsible for a good deal of upward socioeconomic mobility.[57] Although the majority of Mexican-Americans in Los Angeles after 1848 lived in nuclear or extended families, the modified extended family was also a factor in economic mobility.

Far more important than the number of relatives who lived in the home was the system of godparents and compadres called "compadrazgo." Compadrazgo operated as a kinship system uniting the family with the larger society. At the important landmarks of a child's life, the parents asked persons from outside the family to be godparents. These padrinos were almost never blood relatives but respected friends of the family. Since at least two godparents were given at birth,

---

to prove this point by Walter Glazer of the University of Pittsburgh. Glazer points out that Sennett did not consider other variables that might have influenced mobility. He also argues that Sennett's sample of extended families was too small to warrant the conclusion that they were more upwardly mobile than nuclear families. See Walter S. Glazer's review of Sennett's book in the February 1972 *Journal of American History*.

57. Some of those who have developed the concept of the modified extended family and have shown its relation to upward mobility are: William Good, "Family and Mobility," in Reinhard Bendix and Seymour Martin Lipset (eds.), *Class, Status and Power: Social Stratification in Comparative Perspective;* Elaine Cumming and David Schneider, *A Social Profile of Detroit,* and "Sibling Solidarity: A Property of American Kinship," *Am. Anthropologist;* Aamon Firth, *Two Studies of Kinship in London;* Kay Richards Broshard, "Social Class, Occupational Mobility, Migration and Nuclear Family Relations: A Study of the Nuclear Family's Use of Help" (Ph.D. diss.).

confirmation, first communion, and marriage, a child might have as many as eight sets of padrinos, or sixteen persons, who were morally obligated to act as guardians and substitute parents. Once a godparent had agreed to serve, he was expected to render financial assistance when needed and to take the place of the parents if they died.[58]

Compadrazgo was recognized by the Church in a formal ceremony and, in the words of Ygnacio Coronel, it produced a "cord of affection between the father and mother and the godparents."[59] Just how much economic aid compadres gave one another is impossible to determine, but, if contemporary rural practices are any indication, it is probable that these formalized friendships were of considerable economic importance.[60]

Prior to the Mexican War in 1845, about 71 percent of the Angelenos lived in extended families (see Table 24). About 22 percent lived in nuclear families and the remainder, about 8 percent, lived either alone or in unmarried groups. The social and economic conditions created by the Anglo conquest, along with migrations following the discovery of gold, radically altered this structure, especially after 1850. The proportion of extended families fell—by 1880, less than half of Mexican-American families were so classified—while the proportion of nuclear families increased steadily to about a third of all family types. The backwash immigrations from the gold fields also produced a noticeable rise in the number of single persons in the pueblo during the

58. Coronel, *Cosas de California*, p. 231.

59. ORIGINAL SPANISH: Compadrazgo "era un vínculo de afinidad existente entre la padre y la madre . . . y el padrino y la madrina." *Ibid*.

60. For a detailed analysis of contemporary compadrazgo relationships among the Chicanos in the Southwest, see the following works: Madsen, *The Mexican-Americans of South Texas*, pp. 22–42; Octavio I. Romano, "Donship in a Mexican-American Community in Texas," *Am. Anthropologist*, pp. 970–973; Staples, "The Mexican-American Family."

TABLE 24
Family Types,
1844–1880

	Nuclear		Extended		Single	
1844						
N=232	52	22.4%	162	69.8%	18	7.8%
1850						
N=220	47	21.3	153	69.5	20	9.2
1860						
N=530	144	27.2	261	49.2	125	23.6
1870						
N=545	178	36.6	248	41.6	119	21.8
1880						
N=521	159	30.5	260	49.9	102	19.6

SOURCE: Computer analysis of manuscript census returns.

period from 1860 to 1880. The extended family was on the decline. Was the decline of the extended family related to upward socieconomic mobility? Was it true that those living in smaller families were more successful in advancing economically?

Throughout the decades, those heading extended families tended to be wealthier than those heading nuclear ones. In 1860 and 1870, they owned almost twice as much property as those who were supporting smaller families (see Table 25). In general, the larger the family the better the chances its members had of advancing economically.

Other evidence points to the same conclusion: the extended family had an economic advantage. A study of a sample of 113 families who persisted during two periods—1844 to 1860 and 1860 to 1880—shows that those who came from extended families succeeded more often than those who came from nuclear families. In the first years there was no significant difference in socioeconomic mobility. But later, the extended family members had an advantage. They were always more

TABLE 25

Distribution of Income by Type of Family,
1850–1870

Family type:	$0–500		$501–1000		$1001–5000		$5001–10,000		Over $10,000	
	Extended	Nuclear	Extended	Nuclear	Extended	Nuclear	Extended	Nuclear	Extended	Nuclear
1850 N=327	23.9%	25.3%	1.9%	.8%	4.2%	4.6%	.8%	.6%	1.2%	.2%
1860 N=357	25.9	20.9	2.7	2.0	4.7	2.4	2.7	1.1	2.8	.7
1870 N=167	25.0	20.9	3.6	1.8	12.3	5.5	3.6	0	2.3	1.0

SOURCE: Computer analysis of manuscript census returns.

TABLE 26

Persisting Socioeconomic Mobility by Type of Family, 1844–1880

Family type:	1844–1860 (N=59)						1860–1880 (N=54)					
	Single		Nuclear		Extended		Single		Nuclear		Extended	
Upward mobility[a]	1	33.3%	7	25%	7	25%	0	0%	7	28%	8	28%
Downward mobility[b]	1	33.3	5	18	1	4	3	60	8	43	6	26
Stable[c]	1	33.3	16	57	20	71	2	40	8	29	13	46
Totals	3	99.9	23	100	28	100	5	100	23	100	27	100

SOURCE: Computer analysis of manuscript census returns.

a. Defined as an improvement in occupational or economic status.
b. Defined as worsening in occupational or economic status.
c. No change in socioeconomic status.

able to remain in the same occupational or economic status than were nuclear family members. In both periods, those from nuclear families underwent more downward mobility in proportion to their numbers than did those from larger extended families. By 1880, they were almost twice as likely to decline in status than were those living in extended units (see Table 26).

From this it appears that extended rather than nuclear families were better equipped to survive the turbulent postwar decades. The Ariès–Sennett thesis better fits the Mexican-American family in Los Angeles than do other explanations. But why were mobility and family structure related? The most obvious reason has to do with the superior economic and social resources available to extended families. Many such had more than one source of income: children or relatives who worked. Collectively, more income was available to purchase property, make investments, or see a promising child through school. The large family acted as a kind of insurance corporation for its members, providing a cushion for those who experienced hard times.

Family was but one variable among many affecting economic mobility. The changing economic situation, changes in the range of occupational opportunities, and variations in the political and social climate were also important. But on the whole, the extended family seemed better able to withstand the vicissitudes of social and economic change and ease the transition from the Mexican to the American era.

CHAPTER FOUR

An Emerging Ethnic Consciousness

Sociologists know very little about the ways in which ethnic groups are created. Most historical and sociological research in the last three decades has emphasized the problems of assimilation, stereotyping, and prejudice. Very few have investigated the dynamics of ethnic-group emergence.[1]

A recent argument has been that ethnic identity is the result of Anglo-American colonial oppression. This is the theory of Robert Blauner's internal-colonialism model.[2] Blauner believes that the increasing association of race with class is due to the historic exploitation of nonwhites by whites in the United States. He views collective ethnic mentality as a result of colonization. Nonwhite ethnic minorities have been "brainwashed" into believing themselves inferior to white Americans. A number of Chicano sociologists and historians have developed this theory in relation to the Mexican-American experience in the Southwest. Rudolfo Acuña, Gilberto Lopez y Rivas, and Joan Moore are but a few of a growing number who find this explanation appealing.[3]

1. Two sociologists, Robert Blauner and Randall Collins, concur in this evaluation. See Randall Collins, *Conflict Sociology: Towards an Explanatory Science*, p. 84; and Robert Blauner, *Racial Oppression in America*.

2. Robert Blauner, "Internal Colonization and Ghetto Revolt," *Social Problems*.

3. Acuña, *Occupied America*, pp. 1–5; Gilberto Lopez y Rivas, *The Chicanos: Life and Struggles of the Mexican Minority in the United*

Another theory of ethnic emergence is articulated by Randall Collins in his book *Conflict Sociology*. He believes that ethnic consciousness has been created by the historic operation of three conditions: (1) the exclusion of ethnic-group members from the economic mainstream; (2) control of the political and economic institutions by the dominant majority; and (3) visible differences in ethnic cultures and skin colors.[4] Collins holds that ethnic groups emerge as self-conscious entities by an inevitable process of stratification, regardless of the political system. While Blauner believes that ethnic identity is linked to the process of neo-colonial oppression, Collins would say that this consciousness is the result of conflicts within the social system.

Another perspective on the problem comes from social psychologists Tamotsu Shibutani and Kian Kwan.[5] Their approach has been to view ethnic consciousness in terms of the psychodynamics of the ethnic group itself, discounting the influence of the economic or political environment. The emergence of ethnicity, they believe, is dependent upon (1) the degree to which a group maintains its own communication channels (language, press, associations); (2) the degree of shared understandings among the members of the group (consensus); and (3) the extent to which the group can develop social structures to deal with changing life conditions.[6]

Another view has been advanced by historian David Weber. He argues that Anglo-American racial prejudice is at the root of the progressive isolation of Mexican-Americans as a subgroup.[7] Anti-Mexican prejudice, he argues, was directly related to the anti-Catholic, anti-

---

States, pp. 75–82; Joan W. Moore, "Colonization and the Mexican-Americans," *Social Problems.*

4. Collins, *Conflict Sociology,* pp. 84–86.

5. Tamotsu Shibutani and Kian W. Kwan, *Ethnic Stratification: A Comparative Approach.*

6. *Ibid.,* pp. 572–578.

7. David J. Weber (ed.), *Foreigners in Their Native Land,* pp. 52–61.

Spanish *Leyenda Negra* first articulated in northern Europe in the sixteenth century. Economic differences and psychological projective mechanisms also served to increase racism. Anglo-Americans first encountered rude frontier villages on New Spain's northern frontier. From these contacts they assumed that all Mexicans lived in backward conditions. They also projected their own unacceptable feelings onto their hosts. Thus prejudiced from the beginning, Anglos felt justified in creating oppressive and discriminatory economic and social conditions for Mexicans in the Southwest.

I do not take issue with any one of the theories of ethnic emergence summarized above, but have drawn from each a degree of direction in this chapter. There were probably numerous historical variations in the emergence of ethnic consciousness for Mexican-Americans in the Southwest. Each region, city, and colonia developed a unique identity. The result has been a diverse ethnic group.

Violence

In the second half of the nineteenth century, violence made many Mexican-Americans aware of their new status as a separate ethnic group. Lynchings, murders, kangaroo trials, riots, and robberies involving Anglos and Mexican-Americans made both groups aware of their cultural differences.

In the early years, the landholding Californios sided with the Anglo-Americans in condemning racial violence and banditry. But later, as the patterns of conflict became more fixed, they rose to defend La Raza and condemned the racism of the Anglos. The division of the Mexican-American community into lawless and respectable elements gradually lessened as the Spanish-speaking discovered a common meeting ground in Mexican nationalism.

Los Angeles in the 1850's had a reputation as one of the most violent and lawless towns in California. Despite its small population, the pueblo had the highest murder rate in the nation for a time. In 1851–52, there were at least 44 homicides, not counting Indians, found along Calle de los Negros, or "Nigger Alley" as it was called by the Anglos. During 1853–54, Los Angeles averaged about one murder per day.[8] The majority of these crimes went unnoted and unpunished: in total, there were 40 legal executions for murder and 37 lynchings between 1854 and 1870.[9] Most of the lynchings and executions were of Mexican-Americans and Indians accused of murdering Anglos. In 1852, Doroteo Zavaleta and Jesús Rivas were lynched for the murder of an Anglo cattle buyer. That same year, three more Mexican-Americans were lynched for the murder of Joshua Bean. One of the first legal trials for murder in Los Angeles was that of Feliz Alvitre, convicted of murdering a Yankee in 1855.[10]

The bloody chronicle of racial warfare in Los Angeles in the 1850's has been compiled by others. Rather than retrace the details of this violent story, I will focus on some of the major events that seem to have increased the ethnic consciousness of the Mexican-Americans.[11]

The murder trial of Chico and Menito Lugo in 1851 first introduced the *gente de razón* to what they might expect from American justice. The Lugo boys were sons of the wealthy José Maria Lugo, owner of Rancho San Bernardino. Although the Lugo family was highly respected among the Spanish-speaking, this did not seem to influence the opinions of the Anglos. On their way to court, the two boys had to be protected from a lynch mob by an army guard. Leading the mob of

8. Pitt, "The Submergence of the Mexican in California 1846–1890" (Ph.D. diss.), pp. 340–346; Laurence L. Hill, *La Reina: Los Angeles in Three Centuries*, p. 45.

9. Hill, *La Reina*, p. 43.

10. Pitt, *Decline of the Californios*, pp. 156–160.

11. The best chronicles of this violent period in Los Angeles history are to be found in the following works: Pitt, *Decline*, ch. 9; Pitt, "Submergence"; Bell, *Reminiscences of a Ranger*; Benjamin Hayes, *Pioneer Notes, 1849–1875*.

angry Anglo citizens was the desperado Captain John (Red) Irving. He had heard of the trial and had drifted into town with the hope of extorting money from the elder Lugo. Failing in their extortion attempt and then in the lynching, Irving and his gang attempted to kill the Lugos after they had been released from jail on bond. But the plot backfired. The bandit leader and his men were wiped out by Indians. Later, after the case had been dismissed for violation of due process, Solomon Pico, nephew of the last Mexican governor, tried to assassinate the prosecutor, Judge Benjamin Hayes. This attempt to avenge the sullied honor of the Lugo family only increased the tensions between Mexican-Americans and Anglos. In the Lugo affair, Mexican-Americans got a taste of the lynching proclivities of their Anglo neighbors. They began to question the reality of their equal protection under American law.[12]

If the Lugo case had not been warning enough, successful lynchings the next year confirmed Mexican-American doubts. On April 3, 1852, Savaleta and Rivas were lynched. A few months later a vigilante group captured Reyes Feliz and Cipriano Sandoval, charged them with murder, and hung them.[13] Later both Feliz and Sandoval were proved innocent. In later years lynchings continued to terrorize the Mexican-American community. As late as 1892, Francisco Torres was lynched in Santa Ana; and the following year Jesús Cuen was lynched in San Bernardino.[14] Outrage over "los lynchamientos" peppered editorials in the Spanish-language press condemning them as barbaric acts. The editor of *Las Dos Repúblicas* wrote: "It is incredible that a country such as this, which calls itself the center of

12. William W. Robinson, *The People vs. Lugo,* pp. 5–6, and passim.

13. Pitt, "Submergence," p. 346; John W. Caugey (ed.), *The Indians of Southern California in 1852,* pp. xvi–xviii.

14. *Las Dos Repúblicas,* Aug. 23, 1892; April 9, 1893. For a detailed account of the Torres lynching, see Jean F. Riss, "The Lynching of Francisco Torres," *J. Mex.-Am. Hist.*

universal civilization, commits barbaric acts like those which we have related."[15] And later he wrote: "That a civilized people . . . is converted into voluntary assassins deprecating the authorites . . . is really repugnant and a scandal. . . . Our race ought to open their eyes to the light of the truth and see what we can hope from the justice of our friendly cousins."[16]

Mexican Americans did not have equal protection under the law: their language, racial appearance, and "foreign culture" made them criminally suspect, if not guilty, regardless of the sweeping guarantees of the Treaty of Guadalupe Hidalgo and the U.S. Constitution. The disparity between promise and reality at times created insurrectionary situations. Such a case grew out of the murder of Antonio Ruiz in July 1856.

Deputy Constable William W. Jenkins shot and killed Antonio Ruiz when Ruiz had resisted being evicted from his house. The news of the murder mobilized the "turbulent lower classes" and almost resulted in open warfare between Mexican-Americans and Anglos.[17] Authorities jailed Jenkins briefly and then released him on bail. Within a matter of hours, groups of Mexican-Americans held meetings to discuss the situation. The next day, July 20th, 200 to 300 Mexican-Americans from the pueblo and surrounding ranchos formed a posse to re-arrest Jenkins. Interpreting this posse as an insurrection, Anglo citizens called out the army for protection. Groups of Texans, most of them

15. ORIGINAL SPANISH: "Es increible que un país como este, que se dice ser el foco de la civilización universal, se cometan actos de barbarie como el que acabamos de dar cuenta." Las Dos Repúblicas, April 9, 1893. For other reactions to the continued lynchings of Chicanos, see La Revista Hispano-Americana, Aug. 29, 1892.

16. ORIGINAL SPANISH: "Que un pueblo civilizado . . . se converta en asesino voluntario y despreciando las autoridades . . . es realmente repugnante y escandoloso. . . . Nuestra raza en general debe abris los ojos a la luz de la verdad y ver lo que pueden esperar de la justicia de nuestros amables primos." Las Dos Repúblicas, April 9, 1893.

17. Hayes, Pioneer Notes, p. 109; El Clamor Público, Aug. 23, 1856.

ex-Texas Rangers from nearby El Monte, rode into town to help defend the city. At this point Francisco Ramirez, the editor of *El Clamor Público,* wrote that "already everyone is preparing for revolution."[18]

But the Mexican-Americans were divided into two factions: those of the lower classes who were friends of Ruiz and wanted revenge, and the Californios who were trying to mediate the situation. In effect, the community split along the same lines that it had during the Varela revolt in 1846. Andrés Pico, Tomás Sanchez, Antonio Coronel, Augustín Olvera, and Cristobal Aguilar, all members of the upper classes, sided with the Anglos in searching out the leaders of the insurrection. Later they helped organize a vigilante group called the City Guards, which became Los Angeles' first police force.[19]

The split in the ranks of the Mexican-Americans and the capture of the insurrection's leader, Fernando Carriaga, effectively defused the volatile situation. But as Ramirez noted, "the disorder only served to build up the barriers that have for so long existed between the two races."[20]

Less than a year later, Los Angeles was again plunged into insurrectionary turmoil, this time by the depredations of the bandit Juan Flores. Flores was a quasi-revolutionary of the same sort as Joaquin Murieta and Tiburcio Vasquez. Like these bandits, Flores operated with the support of some working-class Mexican-American families who were anxious to be rid of Anglo domination. Flores was not a full-fledged revolutionary but, in Eric Hobsbawm's term, a primitive rebel. He had no ideology, little formal organization, and was more an anarchist than a social reformer.

18. *El Clamor Público,* July 26, 1856.

19. Thompson, West, and Wilson, *History of Los Angeles County,* p. 94; *Los Angeles News,* July 26, 1856.

20. ORIGINAL SPANISH: "El desorden que tuvo lugar el martes solo ha servido para poner más y más distantes los barreros que por mucho tiempo existian entre las dos razas." *El Clamor Público,* July 26, 1856.

Flores' real importance was that he generated heroic legends symbolizing the daily struggles of the Spanish-speaking.[21]

Flores took over Mission San Juan Capistrano in 1857 and from there terrorized the south counties. Rumors spread that Mexican-Americans in Los Angeles were planning an alliance with him, proposing to take over the city.[22] A few weeks later Flores and his men ambushed a local posse. Sheriff Barton and three of his deputies were killed. The road to Los Angeles lay open. Immediately, prominent Anglo and Californio leaders organized a vigilante committee and again called on the El Monte Boys. They declared martial law and surrounded the barrio, where it had been reported that some of Flores' men were hiding. Without warrants or warning, the vigilante group entered houses in the dead of night and rounded up persons whom they suspected of pro-Flores sentiments.[23] A few days later they captured Flores and 52 of his men. They immediately hung him. Later remnants of his band were also caught and lynched without trial.[24]

As in the Ruiz incident a year before, the Mexican-Americans split into two factions. Prior to the expedition to San Juan Capistrano, Flores and his band had spent a few days in Los Angeles, where they had mingled with the poorer classes and gained succor and recruits.[25] According to one observer, Harris Newmark, the poorer classes—mostly Sonorans and recent Spanish-speaking immigrants from other states—were sympathetic to Flores and helped him elude capture.[26]

21. This evaluation of Flores is similar to one by Pedro Castillo and Albert Camarillo (eds.), *Furia y Muerte: Los Bandidos Chicanos.*

22. See the confession of Jesús Espinosa in *El Clamor Público,* Feb. 21, 1857.

23. Newmark and Newmark (eds.), *Sixty Years in Southern California,* p. 207.

24. Thompson, West, and Wilson, *History,* p. 82; *Los Angeles Star,* Feb. 21, 1857.

25. Bell, *Reminiscences,* p. 404.

26. Newmark and Newmark, *Sixty Years,* p. 207.

9. A young teamster hauling wood for the city.
Courtesy of the California Historical Society, Los
Angeles.

10. Calle de los Negros or "Nigger Alley," as it appeared in 1882, scene of much of the violence taking place during the height of racial tensions in the 1850's. Courtesy of the Huntington Library.

The Californios, however, condemned Flores and aided in his capture. Tomás Sanchez was elected sheriff for his part in putting down the Flores rebellion, and Andrés Pico—who himself had once led attacks on American troops during the Mexican War—rode beside the Texas Rangers to help ferret out the bandits.

Ramirez expressed the sentiments of the upper classes when he sought to reduce tensions between Mexican-Americans and Anglos. He wrote: "Race war—the idea is ridiculous—if only rational men calmly look around them in Los Angeles and see how our society is composed."[27] At the same time, Ramirez thought that the Spanish-speaking should stop calling themselves Californios—now a term sullied by association with violence: "With all our hearts we desire to forget this last vestige of distinction," he wrote, hoping that the Spanish-speaking would find relief from racial discrimination by supporting laws and their firm administration.[28]

Banditry did not end with the Flores episode, but continued throughout the 'fifties and 'sixties. One of the most famous of the local bandits, the last of any major significance, was Tiburcio Vasquez. Like Flores and the others, Vasquez split the community into factions. Less romanticized than the legendary Joaquin Murieta, whose life will probably always be shrouded in mystery, Vasquez's exploits are well documented.[29]

27. ORIGINAL SPANISH: "La guerra de los razas—la idea es ridicula—si los hombres racionales miran con calma a su rededor en Los Angeles, y ven como compone nuestra sociedad." *El Clamor Público,* May 29, 1857.

28. ORIGINAL SPANISH: "Deseariámos de todo corazón que se abliese el último vestigio de la distinción que complica esta expresión." *El Clamor Público,* Feb. 21, 1857.

29. Ernest May, "Tiburcio Vasquez," *Q. Hist. Soc. So. Calif.* Vasquez became a literary legend soon after his death, when three San Francisco newspaper reporters wrote romanticized versions of his life: Major Ben C. Trumen, George A. Beers, and Eugene T. Sawyer. For the most complete and scholarly study of the outlaw, see Robert Greenwood and George A. Beers, *The California Outlaw: Tiburcio Vasquez.*

In some respects, his career followed that of Murieta. His hideout was La Cantua Canyon, the same as Murieta's. Both bandits had large followings and generated fierce loyalties and hatreds. Both had the support of the rural campesinos, and both were captured on the verge of staging full-scale insurrections.

Tiburcio Vasquez began his career by escaping from a lynch mob after he had been accused of killing a sheriff in what he described as "an affair of honor." He believed he had been unjustly accused, but continued his outlawry because "certain disgusts and injustices obliged me to embrace the career."[30] Vasquez had the reputation of being generous with his loot as well as being a ladies' man. When he finally was captured and awaited trial, most of his visitors were women who wanted to see if he was as handsome as his legend suggested.

In 1874, Vasquez made his appearance in the Los Angeles region. After a few robberies, the *Los Angeles Express* began accusing the Spanish-speaking community of harboring the bandit. *La Crónica* responded that this was not true and that only a few families were involved with Vasquez—most of them living in the countryside.[31] The Californios were alarmed, fearing that Vasquez would ignite a powder keg of racial violence. The editors of *La Crónica* wrote: "The capture of Vasquez is now a real necessity for our state. . . . The effort to free society of this danger should be unanimous."[32]

Vasquez was able to elude capture as long as he stayed in the rural areas. Eventually, however, he was betrayed and captured, in April 1874. While in jail, waiting to be transported north to stand trial for murder, he granted a local newspaperman a rare interview. He re-

30. ORIGINAL SPANISH: "Ciertos disgustos y malos tratamientos me obligaron a abrazar la carrera." *La Crónica,* March 7, 1874.

31. *La Crónica,* May 2, 1874.

32. ORIGINAL SPANISH: "La captura de Vasquez es ya para nuestro estado una verdadera necesidad. . . . Debe ser unánime el esfuerzo para librar a la sociedad de ese peligro." *La Crónica,* April 22, 1874.

lated his life's story along with an apology for his past deeds and a warning to the Spanish-speaking community. Above all he pleaded with his followers not to seek revenge.[33] But his warning went unheeded. A few weeks after his execution a man named Romo shot and killed two Anglos who had been involved in his capture. Immediately an Anglo lynch mob captured and hung Romo. This incident threatened to erupt into wider violence as groups of armed Mexican-Americans met secretly and talked of revenge. Nothing more transpired, however, due largely to the concerted efforts of the upper classes, who were anxious to prevent a renewal of conflict.[34]

Discrimination

There were more subtle ways in which the majority made the Spanish-speaking aware of a new minority status. In 1855 the State Legislature passed a number of arbitrary laws aimed directly at controlling the Mexican-Americans' way of life. A Sunday Law imposed fines ranging from 10 to 500 dollars for engaging in "barbarous or noisy amusements" which were listed as bullfights, horse races, cockfights, and other traditional Californio amusements. At the same time, a vagrancy law called "The Greaser Law" was passed by the Legislature. This law imposed fines and jail sentences on unemployed Mexican-Americans who, at the discretion of local authorities, could be called "vagrants."[35] These new Anglo-American laws reflected the ascendency in Northern California of the Know-Nothing Party (Los Ignorantes).

In response to these restrictive and racist laws, Ramirez wrote scathing editorials denouncing their intent. Other Mexican-Americans, most of them mem-

33. Interview with Vasquez reported in Richard G. Mitchell, "Joaquin Murieta: A Study of Special Conditions in Early California" (Master's thesis), fn. p. 66.

34. See *La Crónica*, June 13, 1874, for an account of the aftermath of Vasquez's execution.

35. *California Statutes*, 1855, cited in Pitt, *Decline*, pp. 197, 220.

bers of the respected classes, favored these strict laws. They wrote letters to Ramirez arguing that such restrictions were necessary to curb the rampant lawlessness of the pueblo.[36] Strict regulations concerning the Sabbath were not new to the Californios. The Mexican ayuntamiento had passed similar laws as early as 1838, but these had always been selectively enforced and were primarily aimed at the Indian population.[37] In 1858 the Legislature repealed these statutes; but in 1860 Los Angeles passed municipal codes prohibiting bullfights and regulating fiestas.[38]

Mexican Americans were more directly affected by the lack of competent Spanish-speaking lawyers and jurors. Underrepresentation and misrepresentation in the judicial process made true justice hard to come by in Los Angeles. Efforts were made to remedy the language problem in the courts by appointing Manual Clemente Rojo, Louis Robidoux and Jonathan Scott as court translators. But according to Harris Newmark, who spoke Spanish and who often attended court, their translations were usually distorted and biased.[39] Upper-class Mexican-Americans were represented on the bench. These judges, from old-line Californio families, had little sympathy with the lower classes. Augustín Olvera served as a county judge until 1853. In 1863 Pablo de la Guerra was elected judge of the Southern District Court, and after 1873 Ygnacio Sepúlveda served as a judge for this same court.[40]

There were no Mexican-American lawyers in the pueblo prior to 1872 when José R. Ramirez began a practice in partnership with a man named Stanford.[41]

---

36. *El Clamor Público,* July 24, 1855; April 19, 1856.

37. James M. Guinn, "The Old Pueblo Archives," *Q. Hist. Soc. So. Calif.*

38. Bullfighting, although outlawed by municipal ordinance after 1860, continued until 1872, but they did not kill the bull. See Thompson, West, and Wilson, *History,* p. 101.

39. Newmark and Newmark, *Sixty Years,* p. 56.

40. W. W. Robinson, *The Lawyers of Los Angeles,* p. 45.

41. *La Crónica,* July 3, 1875.

Economic hardships and educational deprivations excluded many Mexican-Americans from the practice of law. A few lawyers from Mexico found their way into the pueblo and set up practice. Not until the late 1880's did any native-born Mexican-American lawyers emerge. During the period 1887–1900, out of 194 men admitted to the bar in California, only 3 were Spanish-surnamed.[42]

Mexican-Americans suffered juridical inequality and underrepresentation in other ways. They were conspicuously absent on local juries (see Table 27). During the 1860's and 1870's, the proportion of Mexican-Americans who served on grand and trial juries was far below their proportion in the general population. By 1873 Spanish-surnamed individuals were almost completely excluded. Although they comprised more than 30 percent of the city's population, only 2 percent served on juries.

Mexican-Americans were also excluded from the federal juries which met in Los Angeles beginning in 1887. Out of more than 2,000 persons who served as jurors for the Federal District Court during the period 1887–1896, only 8 were Spanish-surnamed. Further research by others has established that this trend of exclusion continued into the twentieth century.[43]

Due to the small number of Spanish-surnamed lawyers and trial jurors, it is not surprising to find large numbers of Mexican-Americans convicted of crimes. In 1856, for example, more than half of those sentenced for major crimes in Los Angeles were Spanish-surnamed.[44] After 1880, Mexican-Americans represented less than 19 percent of the city's population.

42. "Rolls of Attorneys from June 13, 1887, to November 9, 1925" (ms., Federal Records Center, Los Angeles).

43. U.S. District Court, Southern Section, "Jury Roll, 1887–1896," vol. 1; see also Regan R. Garcia, "Archives Report, March 15, 1971" (both mss., Federal Records Center, Los Angeles). Garcia found that of the 240 jurors serving the District Court in 1912, only 13 had Spanish surnames.

44. Pitt, "Submergence," p. 343; *Los Angeles Star,* Aug. 9, 1856.

TABLE 27
Mexican-American Participation on Juries,
1863–1873[a]

	Number of Mexican-American jurors	Total number of jurors	Percentage of city's population Mexican-American	Percentage of city's juries Mexican-American
1863	20	151	58%[b]	13%
1864	57	230		25
1865	n.d.	n.d.		n.d.
1866	72	172		45
1867	n.d.	n.d.		n.d.
1868	n.d.	n.d.		n.d.
1869	n.d.	n.d.		n.d.
1870	60	300	37[c]	20
1871	55	300		19
1872	n.d.	n.d.		n.d.
1873	5	300		2

SOURCE: "Lists of Grand and Trial Jurors, 1863–1873" (m.s., Box 573, L.A. County Mus. Nat. Hist.).
n.d. = no data available.
a. Grand and trial jurors only.
b. According to manuscript census returns for 1860.
c. According to manuscript census returns for 1870.

Throughout the state they were probably no more than 1 percent of the total.[45] During the period 1887–1890, however, more than 22 percent of those convicted of federal crimes by the District Court of Los Angeles were Spanish-surnamed. In Los Angeles county alone,

45. The exact numbers of Mexican-Americans within the state during the nineteenth century will probably never be known, since the census did not distinguish between persons with Spanish surnames or of Mexican ancestry and the general population. Bancroft estimated that in 1848 there were about 7,500 Californios living in the state. Allowing that the Spanish-surnamed population of California increased at the same rate as did the pueblo's Spanish population, we may estimate that by 1890 the total Mexican-American population probably numbered between 13,000 and 15,000. The

for the year of 1887, almost 30 percent of those convicted of criminal offenses were Mexican-Americans.[46]

Mexican-Americans knew that they received unequal treatment under the law. In 1878, for example, Julian Rodriguez, editor of *El Eco de la Patria,* complained that "the least small offence committed by one of our compatriots attracts the total weight of the law."[47] He cited the example of an Anglo who was convicted of murdering a Mexican-American and was sentenced to only one year in jail—eventually this man served 70 days of his sentence. In the same year, a Mexican-American who was convicted of disorderly conduct was given a 90-day jail term. It was clear that this unequal treatment was racial prejudice of a systematic type. That the courts treated Mexican-Americans as a special group reinforced La Raza's sense of ethnic separateness.

Repatriation

Mexican-Americans reacted against the intolerable social and economic conditions created by the Anglo-American conquest by organizing expeditions to return to Mexico and found colonies. They had little financial help from the Mexican government in these ventures, yet many of the groups were successful in settling California repatriates.[48] Some of those who returned to

---

state population in 1890 was 1,213,398. Thus Mexican-Americans in that census year probably represented about 1 percent of the total state population.

46. For the period 1887–1890, 16 out of 46 persons convicted by the District Court had Spanish surnames. The District Court heard cases for Southern California, south of San Luis Obispo. For 1887, 17 out of 56 persons convicted by the county courts were Spanish-surnamed. U.S. District Court, Southern Section, "Register of Criminal Cases, 1887–1905," (ms., Federal Records Center, Los Angeles); Los Angeles County Clerk's Office, Superior Court, Criminal Division, "Criminal Complaints, 1887."

47. ORIGINAL SPANISH: "La mas pequeña falta cometida por uno de nuestro compatriotas atrae todo el peso de la ley." *El Eco de la Patria,* Feb. 21, 1878.

48. The Mexican government did send commissioners to help repatriate Mexican-Americans, but they were frustrated by American authorities. See David Weber, *Foreigners,* pp. 142–143.

Mexico were miners who had come to California during the Gold Rush. But there were also large numbers of native-born Californios who were anxious to improve their lives in a more friendly country.

The first period of repatriation lasted until 1880, when the Mexican central government began to formulate a specific plan for the return of former Mexican citizens. Under the stern guidance of the dictator Porfirio Díaz, the government attempted to encourage foreigners as well as Mexican-Americans to settle in Mexico. This was part of a plan to encourage the industrialization of the country. During the two decades prior to the Mexican Revolution of 1910, foreign immigrants, including Anglo-Americans, Frenchmen, and Mexican-Americans, established small colonias in remote and underdeveloped regions of the republic. Altogether, about 31,000 Mexican-Americans migrated back to Mexico. The largest numbers came after 1880, when the Mexican National Railroad, linking El Paso with Mexico City, was completed.[49] The number of repatriates in the four decades after the conquest was about 25 percent of the total Mexican-American population of the Southwest in 1850.[50] That more did not emigrate to Mexico can be explained by the fact that the vast majority of Mexican-Americans prior to 1910 were living in their native land. Understandably, they were slow to abandon their homes for the dangers of a foreign environment.

It is not surprising that one of the first recorded repatriation societies was formed in Los Angeles in 1855 during the height of racial conflict and violence. In that year, *La Estrella,* the Spanish-language section of the *Los Angeles Star,* announced the formation of La Sociedad de Colonización de Nativos de California para el Estado de Sonora (The Colonization Society of

49. Moises Gonzales Navarro, *La Colonizacion de Mexico, 1877–1910,* p. 56.

50. See Martinez, "On the Size of the Chicano Population," *Aztlán,* pp. 43–67.

Native Californians for the State of Sonora). Andrés
Pico and other members of the Californios helped organize this society.[51] Later the group disbanded, as
other colonization societies captured the interest of the
pueblo.

The same year, 1855, *El Clamor Público* reported the
formation of another society, this one headed by Jesús
Islas from San José. Islas traveled to Sonora to investigate the possibilities of settling large numbers of "Mexican Spanish Americans and Californios." Florencio
Monteverde, Minister of Interior Development at
Hermosillo, expressed his support for the project. The
Sonorans "received the project with great enthusiasm,"
offering donations of cattle and food for the prospec-
tive colonists.[52]

Back in California, Islas organized an expedition and
in September 1856 reached Los Angeles, where he
began recruiting colonists by running advertisements in
the newspapers.[53] In a few days he had recruited almost
300 people. On October 11, 1856, the expedition set
out for northern Mexico.[54] For the next few years, the
fate of the Islas expedition was a frequent topic of con-
versation in the pueblo. Mexican-Americans learned
that the colonists had arrived in Sonora without mis-
hap, that they had been given thirty-acre parcels of
land, formerly parts of Mission Soric, and that other
Californio migrants were joining them daily. By 1858
it appeared that this colonization venture was succeeding. Islas reported, "We are living very peacefully and
breathing the pure and agreeable air of this beautiful
climate."[55]

51. *La Estrella,* March 15, 1855.
52. ORIGINAL SPANISH: "El projecto ha sido recibido con gran en-
tusiasmo para todas las pobulaciones del estado." *El Clamor Público,*
Feb. 16, 1856.
53. *Ibid.,* Sept. 6, 1856.
54. *Ibid.,* Oct. 4, 1856.
55. ORIGINAL SPANISH: "Vivimos muy tranquilos y respirando el
aire puro y agradable de este hermosa clima." *El Clamor Público,* Oct.
2, 1858.

Islas' success spurred others to imitation. In October 1858 a group of Mexican-Americans formed La Junta para Promover la Emigración de Todos los Hispanos-Americanos Residentes en California (The Steering Committee to Promote Immigration of All Spanish-Americans Living in California).[56] They made clear that their major purpose was to escape the inhospitable social and economic climate of Anglo-dominated California. In their promotional literature they lauded the beauties of the Sonoran climate and the potential wealth of the Mexican nation: "The tranquility of Sonora is the salvation of the Spanish-Americans who live in California," they wrote.[57] La Junta seemed to have more representatives from working-class Mexican-Americans than earlier organizations. Manuel Retes, the president, and most of the other officers were relatively unknown to the *gente de razón*. Nevertheless, this did not mean that their purposes were at odds with the desires of the upper class. Francisco Ramirez, who usually echoed the sentiments of the respectable elements, devoted a front page of his newspaper to La Junta. He encouraged Mexican-Americans to join: "conditions of the Hispano-Americans in California, far from having improved, have worsened," and he went on to suggest that emigration was a desirable way of escaping a deteriorating situation.[58] *El Eco del Pacifico,* a radical newspaper in San Francisco, also endorsed La Junta's project, expressing the hope that colonization would "improve the condition of the proletarian class of our people."[59]

La Junta later sent two representatives to Mexico to negoiate with the government of Sonora. They reached an agreement whereby the governor promised

56. *Ibid.,* Oct. 16, 1858.
57. ORIGINAL SPANISH: "La tranquilidad de Sonora es la salvación de los Hispano-Americanos que viven en California." *El Clamor Público,* Oct. 16, 1858.
58. *El Clamor Público,* Nov. 13, 1858.
59. ORIGINAL SPANISH: " . . . mejorar la suerte de la clase proletaria de nuestra raza." *Ibid.*

to pay for the transportation of the immigrants and furnish land and capital for the proposed colonia.[60] After 1858 the local newspapers were silent about the fate of La Junta's colony—possibly the venture fell through because of financial or political difficulties.

That the vast majority of Mexican-Americans did not return to Mexico after the conquest suggests that they realized their way of life had become different from that of Mexico. Due to their historic isolation from Mexican society, native-born Mexican-Americans in California, New Mexico, and Texas had evolved distinctly different forms of culture. After 1848 they were neither Mexicans nor Americans, but a marginal people.

On the other hand, the repatriation organizations laid the foundations for an idealized patriotic identification with Mexico. This was a new development. During the Mexican era, the Californios had resisted integration into the Mexican governmental system. Ironically, as a result of Anglo-American domination, the Spanish-speaking of California now looked to Mexico as a spiritual homeland. The Californio newspapers were, almost without exception, enthusiastic about the repatriation movement. As a result of the exhortations of Ramirez and other newspaper editors, Mexico became the promised land.

But the reported experiences of the repatriates made some Los Angeles Mexican-Americans aware of the cultural differences. Accounts of bloody Indian wars and governmental coups discouraged many from going. In some cases, the Mexican government was hostile, turning away Mexican-American immigrants for fear of political repercussions from their citizens.[61] Fearing economic competition, Mexican merchants protested against migration.[62] Some educated Mexicans expressed their fear that the migration of partially

60. *Ibid.*, Nov. 26, 1858.
61. *La Crónica*, April 21, 1883.
62. *El Monitor Mexicano*, Oct. 26, 1895.

Anglicized Mexican-Americans would corrupt their national language and culture. The editors of La Integridad in Mexico City believed that pochismos (Anglicized Spanish) threatened to "corrupt the language . . . and ultimately result in converting us into strangers in our own country."[63]

As a result, Mexico became more a spiritual than a physical homeland for California-born Mexican-Americans. On one hand they were enthusiastic about Mexico's political and economic development. But on the other, they were suspicious about their reception in what had become a foreign country.[64]

Ethnic Newspapers and Organizations

The Spanish-speaking of Los Angeles in the period 1850–1880 were an emerging ethnic group. They spoke a language that excluded the majority population. Most spoke a regional dialect of Spanish. Several newspaper editors made a point of emphasizing that their journals were written in the purest Castilian. This implied that an argot, containing some Americanisms and slang terms, was already forming. Ignacio Sepúlveda, writing to Hubert Howe Bancroft in 1874, lamented the decline of Castilian Spanish among the Californios in Los Angeles.[65] A linguistic analysis of the Spanish written by newspaper editors might perhaps reveal something of the cultural changes taking place. Others who have studied Los Angeles Spanish in the nineteenth and twentieth centuries have noted that Mexican-Americans there have evolved unique linguistic patterns.[66]

63. ORIGINAL SPANISH: " . . . corromper el idioma . . . y último resultado convertirnos en extranjeros en nuestra propria patria." La Integridad editorial, reprinted in La Crónica, Nov. 24, 1883.

64. La Crónica, April 28, 1883, warned that vague promises of land grants by the Mexican government should be regarded with caution. La Revista Hispano-Americana, Dec. 6, 1892, said that the Mexican government might not welcome Californio repatriados, since they were technically American citizens.

65. Ignacio Sepúlveda to Hubert Howe Bancroft, July 9, 1874 (ms.) (Bancroft Library).

66. See Robert N. Phillips, "Los Angeles Spanish: A Descriptive

The rapid growth of a Spanish-speaking press is further evidence that Mexican-Americans were forging a new social identity. The social distance which at first separated the Californios from the common man decreased, not only through the economic leveling of the upper classes, but also through a democratization of the printed means of communication.

In the Spanish and Mexican periods, Los Angeles had no newspapers. There had been little need for them, since the pueblo was small. Few could read, and few had interests outside their immediate localities. During the American era all of this changed. Suddenly Los Angeles' population grew, almost tripling in ten years. Literacy became more widespread, and the Spanish-speaking took more interest in outside affairs. There followed a journalistic revolution, as at least 16 Spanish-language newspapers made their appearances in the pueblo before the turn of the century. This was not just a local phenomenon but part of a movement among Mexican-Americans throughout the Southwest.[67] Table 28 lists Spanish-language newspapers for Los Angeles in the nineteenth century, along with the names of their editors and known dates of publication.

The Spanish-language press reflected a diversity of opinion, but in general there were two main types of newspapers. One reflected the opinions and concerns of the native-born Californios. Representatives of this Californio press were *La Estrella, El Clamor Público, La*

Analysis" (Ph.D. diss.); Antonio S. Blanco, *La Lengua Española en la Historia de California.*

67. Herminio Ríos has found that between 1850 and 1970 over 500 Mexican-American papers were founded. C. Herminio Ríos, "Towards a True Chicano Bibliography," *El Grito,* pp. 38–43. Literature dealing with the Spanish-language press in Los Angeles is noticeably scanty; but some useful works are: Muir Dawson, "Southern California Newspapers, 1851–1856," *Q. Hist. Soc. So. Calif.;* Thompson, West, and Wilson, *History,* p. 77; and Robert E. Park, *The Immigrant Press and Its Social Control,* and "The Foreign Language Press and Social Progress," in Robert E. Park and Herbert A. Miller, *On Social Control and Collective Behavior,* pp. 133–144.

TABLE 28

Spanish-Language Newspapers in Los Angeles,
1850–1900

Name of paper	Publishers and editors	Dates of publication
1. *La Estrella*	Manuel C. Rojo	1851–1855
2. *El Clamor Público*	José É. Gonzales	1855–1859
	Francisco Ramirez	
3. *El Amigo del Pueblo*	José E. Gonzales	1861–1866
4. *La Crónica*	E. F. Teodoli	1872–1892
	Francisco Ramirez	
	Pastor de Celis	
	M. J. Varela	
	S. A. Cardona	
	E. F. de Celis	
5. *La Verdad*	unknown	1870's
6. *La Voz de la Juventud*	unknown	1876
7. *La Voz de la Justicia*	unknown	1876
8. *El Joven*	A. Cuyas	1877–1878
	José F. Rodriguez	
9. *El Eco de la Patria*	Alberto Gallando	1878
	Julían Rodrequez	
10. *El Aguacero*	Ramón Gonzales	1878
	Luis Romero	
11. *El Demócrata*	Juan de Toro	1882
12. *La Fe en la*		
Democracia	Juan de Toro	1884
13. *El Eco Mexicano*	José G. de Vega	1885
	José M. Obrando	
14. *La Revista Hispano*		
Americana	Manuel Sánchez	1882–1894
	H. D. Barrows	
The Spanish		
American Review	A. Cuyas	
(bilingual)		
15. *Las Dos Repúblicas*	Pastor de Celis	1892–1898
	Miguel J. Varela	
	E. F. de Celis	
	S. A. Cardona	
	Tomás Temple	
	A. J. Flores	
	E. Olivas	
16. *El Monitor Mexicano*	E. Olivas	1895

SOURCE: All of these papers are available in broken series in the Los Angeles County Museum of Natural History. The most complete collection of *El Clamor Público* is in the Huntington Library.

Crónica, and *Las Dos Repúblicas.* Because they were financed and supported by the wealthiest members of the community, these newspapers were long-lived and influential. *Las Dos Repúblicas,* for example, had branch offices throughout the state, as well as in Arizona and in northern Mexico. *La Crónica* was incorporated and had facilities for statewide distribution.

The second type of Mexican-American newspaper gave voice to a more populist point of view. *La Voz de la Justicia, El Eco de la Patria,* and *El Eco Mexicano* were of this sort. Most of them had been started by Mexican immigrants with meager resources. They were unable to maintain publication for more than a few years. In general, they tended to express the more nationalistic sentiments of the Spanish-speaking population, especially of those born in Mexico. Gordon Allport, in his study *The Nature of Prejudice,* has argued that one of the results of persecution is the strengthening of group ties: "Within their in-group they can laugh and deride their persecutors, celebrate their own heroes and holidays, · and live quite comfortably. As long as they cohere, they need not feel too much haunted by their problems."[68] The Spanish-language press increased Mexican-Americans' solidarity by reporting common experiences of persecution and discrimination.

The Mexican-American press took the lead in condemning lynchings and job discrimination. Editors also sought to arouse community concern about the land issue and racial prejudice. *El Clamor Público*'s editor, Francisco Ramirez, was a major leader in protesting Anglo-American theft of California lands. In 1858 he issued a lengthy statement of grievances against Anglo rule under the title "Expreción simultanea del pueblo de California" (The united cry of the people of California). In it Ramirez denounced the "usurpation of lands" and the cultural aggrandizement of the "norteamericanos," and urged "noncomformity with their

68. Gordon Allport, *The Nature of Prejudice,* p. 149.

domination." He listed ten articles of resistance that he hoped would mobilize the community.[69] Later Ramirez castigated the Californios for their lack of concern: "And you, imbecile Californios! You are to blame for the lamentations that we are witnessing. We are tired of saying 'open your eyes,' and it is time that we demand our rights and interests. It is with shame that we say, and difficult to confess it: you are the mockery of humanity!"[70] Ramirez was only one of many editors who sought to awaken the Spanish-speaking to the political and economic meanings of persecution.

In 1877 José Rodriquez, editor of the populist *El Joven*, wrote a lengthy article criticizing the unequal treatment given the residents of Sonora Town by the City Council. He was alarmed that the Anglo members of the Council had proposed destroying Pío Pico's house near the plaza.[71] Pico's house, although in disrepair, held many memories for the Californios. In 1845 it had been the official capital of the province and had been the meeting place of Californio juntas during the 1850's. That the Anglos should regard this monument with such callousness disgusted Rodriguez. Segregation and prejudice also concerned the editors of *La Crónica*, Pastor de Celis, Mariano J. Varela, and S. A. Cardona. In 1877 they observed that the "barrio Latina" had inferior roads and public services. "Why," they asked, "don't they give us the same services that the others have?"[72] They thought the answer lay in the discriminatory neglect of public officials. What was needed was community organization and action: "We still have a

69. *El Clamor Público*, July 24, 1858. See Pitt's *Decline of the Californios*, ch. 9, for a detailed history of this editor and his crusade against the injustices suffered by Mexican-Americans.

70. *El Clamor Público*, Dec. 18, 1858, trans. in Acuña, *Occupied America*, p. 114.

71. *El Joven*, Sept. 18, 1877.

72. ORIGINAL SPANISH: "¿Porqúe, pués no se les extienden por igual los beneficios que se cree mercen a los otros?" *La Crónica*, May 16, 1877.

11. Mexicano caballeros parading down Main Street as part of a fiesta celebration, 1895. Courtesy of the Huntington Library.

12. A panoramic view of Sonora Town in 1879.
Distant view of Southern Pacific Railroad shops.
Courtesy of the Los Angeles Public Library.

voice, tenacity, and rights; we have not yet retired to the land of the dead."[73]

When discrimination took other forms, the editors of *La Crónica* were quick to react. In 1877 a smallpox epidemic broke out. A Doctor Gale appeared before the Common Council and argued that the unsanitary habits of the Mexican-Americans were the source of the contagion. The editors ridiculed this idea in the next day's issue of *La Crónica,* noting that only 21 cases of smallpox had actually been reported and that, while most of them were among the Spanish-speaking, the majority of Mexican-Americans were meticulously following the public health regulations.[74]

In 1882 Juan de Toro, writing in *El Demócrata,* revived the memory of the restrictive Sunday Laws passed by the Common Council in 1860. In de Toro's view, these statutes had been passed by "those who condemn our people, subjecting them to the maxims and principles of a few puritans."[75] De Toro hoped that by supporting the Democratic Party in the next election, Mexican-Americans would be able to repeal these ordinances. The Democrats won the next election, but the laws stayed on the books.

Besides developing ethnic awareness by pointing out group victimization, the Mexican-American press also developed a sense of community in more positive ways. This was especially true in their reporting of Mexican Independence Day celebrations, lasting from September 15th through September 27th (later changed to the 15th and 16th), and the Cinco de Mayo celebration of the defeat of the French forces in Mexico in 1862. They advertised these holidays well in advance and carried detailed accounts of the festivities. Often

73. ORIGINAL SPANISH: "Todavía tenemos voz, tesón y derechos, que no hemos entrado aún en el retiro de los elementos muertos." *Ibid.*

74. *Ibid.,* Jan. 27, 1877.

75. ORIGINAL SPANISH: " . . . quiere condenar a nuestro pueblo a sujetarse a los maximos y principios de un corto número de Puritánicos." *El Demócrata,* Oct. 21, 1882.

they devoted whole pages to an explication of the historical and nationalistic meanings of the celebrations. *Las Dos Repúblicas* sometimes printed its front page as a tricolor of red, green, and white, the Mexican national colors, to celebrate Cinco de Mayo. In 1894 they expounded the ethnic significance of this holiday: "Oh that the God of Peace would pour out his blessings on the people of the same race and bring about a day in which there will be a confederation of the Latin people. . . ."[76]

Early in the 1870's, the populist press took impetus from the nationalistic movement of Benito Juárez. The titles of some of these short-lived newspapers reflected a shift in political awareness: *La Voz de la Justicia* (The Voice of Justice), *El Eco de la Patria* (The Echo from the Homeland), *El Eco Mexicano* (The Mexican Echo). *El Demócrata*'s statement was typical: "We propose, by forming part of the Spanish-language press in California, to defend our interests and to take the forum in the defense of our country which has been so often attacked by our gratuitous enemies."[77]

The editor, Juan de Toro, was one of the first Mexican-American historians. In 1882 he published *A Brief Sketch of the Colonization of California and the Foundation of the Pueblo of Our Lady of Los Angeles* on the occasion of the hundredth anniversary of the founding of the pueblo.[78] His main thesis was that the idea of private property was an evolutionary concept. He traced the history of property through four stages: the Indian, the Spanish, the Mexican, and the Anglo-

---

76. ORIGINAL SPANISH: "Que el Dios de la Paz derrame sus beniciones sobre los pueblos de la misma raza, y que llegue un día en que formandos una gran conferación de la raza latina, puedan estos pasear sus gloriosos estandartes sobre la paz del universo." *Las Dos Repúblicas,* May 5, 1894.

77. ORIGINAL SPANISH: "nos proponemos, al formar parte de la prensa Española de California, defender nuestras intereses, saltar a la palestra en defensa de nuestra patria atacada a menudo por nuestra gratuitas enemigos." *El Eco de la Patria,* Feb. 14, 1878.

78. Los Angeles, Daily Commercial Job Printing House, 1882.

American. By pointing out the relativity of property rights, de Toro was indirectly showing that the Anglo-American claim to the land was not absolute, but part of a historical process.

In his newspapers, *El Demócrata* and *La Fé en la Democracia,* de Toro continued to show how "La Raza Latina" had evolved a consciousness of its unique historical role. In some ways he preceded José Vasconcelos in his visualization of "La Raza Cósmica" that was destined to lead the world to a new era of civilization. In de Toro's view: "The Latin Race has its origin, both human and divine, like the origin of Jesus Christ. It was predestined, embodying the hopes of a race—a glorious race that possesses all the secrets of all the mysteries. . . . This race is falsely accused by these people who don't understand it, because it has more soul than material possessions."[79]

The increasing use of "La Raza" as a generic term in the Spanish-language press was evidence of a new kind of ethnic consciousness. Prior to the Mexican War, the main lines of group cohesiveness were drawn by conflicts with the Mexican authorities. Consequently, Californios had tended to emphasize regional and family loyalties more than loyalty to race or country. After the war with the United States, the tendency was to move from particular allegiances toward a more general group solidarity. This change came about mainly because of Mexican-American conflicts with Anglo-Americans. The Anglos, after all, viewed the Spanish-speaking as a separate race. Consequently the Spanish-speaking were forced to redefine their loyalties in racial terms.

La Raza connoted racial, spiritual, and blood ties with the Latin American people, particularly with

79. ORIGINAL SPANISH: "La Raza Latina tiene su orígen, sino devino, humano, al lado del origen, sino devino, fué predestinado, encarnando las esperanzas de una raza—raza gloriosa que posee todos los secretos de todos los misterios. . . . Raza calumniada por las razas que no la compreden . . . porque tiene más alma que materia." *El Demócrata,* Oct. 18, 1882.

Mexico. And La Raza emerged as the single most important symbol of ethnic pride and identification. There were many ways of using this term, depending on the context. "La Raza Mexicana," "La Raza Hispano-Americana," "La Raza Española," and "La Raza Latina" were all used to convey a sense of the racial, class, and national variety within the Spanish-speaking community. But in general the use of "La Raza" implied membership in a cultural tradition that was separate from the "Anglo-Sajones" or "norte-americanos." In *El Clamor Público*, Francisco Ramirez frequently used the term "nuestra raza" in addressing the Spanish-speaking community.[80] *La Crónica* was dedicated "to the defense of 'La Raza Latin.'"[81] In the 1870's, the editors of *El Joven* published a serial novel called *Los Novedades* which was dedicated to the "pueblos de la raza."[82] *Las Dos Repúblicas* frequently used the term "La Raza Mexicana" or simply "nuestra raza" in their editorials.[83] Thus, regardless of the type of newspaper, "La Raza" came to be a common term of self-identification.

At the same time, a number of social clubs and political associations began to draw the community together and to define the boundaries of cultural and ethnic awareness.[84] Between 1850 and 1900, at least 15 community groups were organized (see Table 29). Most of these were political in purpose, ranging from the conservative Spanish-American Republican Club to the more militant Companía Militar and Los Lanceros. After 1863, the most influential of these organizations

80. *El Clamor Público*, Nov. 18, 1858.
81. *La Crónica*, March 11, 1874.
82. *El Joven*, April 12, 1878.
83. *Las Dos Repúblicas*, Sept. 15, 1897.
84. For an evaluation of the social function of Mexican-American political and social organizations, see Salvador Alvarez, "Mexican-American Community Organizations," *El Grito*. Alvarez argues that Mexican-American organizations have always provided "a vehicle for the expression of the broader boundaries of the communities in which they exist," and that "they have functioned for the preservation of the Mexican way of life."

was La Junta Patriótica de Juárez, a Mexican nationalist organization that sponsored the pueblo's Independence Day and Cinco de Mayo celebrations. The main significance of these groups was that they kept alive a sense of Mexican patriotism and, at the same time, strengthened the local culture.

Before each holiday, La Junta usually organized a parade which preceded the speechmaking and the fiesta. In 1878, during Cinco de Mayo, José J. Carrillo, the Grand Marshal, headed the procession, followed by a band led by Hinlo Silvas. Next came the respected orators of the day—Reginaldo del Valle and Eulegio de Celis, president of La Junta—riding together in a flowered carriage. They were followed by Trinidad Muñoz and Californio representatives of the City Guard carrying the American and the Mexican flags. After them came the 200 members of La Junta Patriótica, followed by Pantelón Zabatela's Guardía Zaragosa. Ten units representing the upper class and other Mexican-American social and political organizations also marched in the parade.[85]

The Cinco de Mayo parade of 1878 showed the changed orientation of the Spanish-speaking community. In Mexican times, most community celebrations had been religious. Certainly members of the upper class had always been the central figures in pueblo celebrations. But in the American era, religion and class became less important, and the community began to emphasize political ideology and ethnic origin. As loyalties ceased to revolve around the Church and the landholders, more abstract sentiments, having to do with Mexican nationalism, began to bind the Spanish-speaking together.

Nonpolitical associations were also important in the life of the community. The labor association, Los Caballeros de Trabajo; the music association, El Club Musical Hispano-Americano; and the Fraternal Order

85. A more detailed description of the day's events can be found in *La Crónica*, Sept. 18, 1878.

TABLE 29
Organizations in Los Angeles,
1850–1900

Name of organization	Earliest named leader	Known date of formation
1. Hijos de Temperancia	unknown	1855
2. Los Lanceros de Los Angeles	Juan Sepúlveda	1857
3. La Junta Patriótica de Juárez (Mexicana)	Juan Prieto	1863–1893
4. La Companía Militar de Rifleros (later La Guardía Zaragosa)	Pantelón Zabaleta	1875
5. La Sociedad Hispano-Americana de Beneficia Mutua	Domingo Garcia	1875–19-?
6. La Junta Guardía Hidalgo	unknown	1877
7. Las Reformistas	Mariano Lugo (sec.)	1877
8. La Corte Colón	Antonio Flores	188?
9. Los Caballeros de Trabajo	unknown	1878
10. La Sociedad Progresista Mexicana	unknown	1883
11. The Spanish-American Republican Club	unknown	1886
12. El Club Politica	Mariano Aguirre	1893

of La Corte Colón attracted Mexican-Americans. The most influential of these cultural organizations was La Sociedad Hispano-Americana de Beneficia Mutua—a mutual-aid society. Throughout the nineteenth and twentieth centuries, privately financed *mutualistas* have operated as self-help agencies, giving loans to

TABLE 29
Organizations in Los Angeles,
1850–1900
(continued)

Name of organization	Earliest named leader	Known date of formation
13. El Club Filar-mónico Mexicano	Ygnacio Perez	1896
14. El Club Musical Hispano-Americano	unknown	1896
15. El Club Estudiantil Hispano-Americano	unknown	1896

SOURCES: References to these organizations can be found prin-cipally in the Spanish-language newspapers published in Los Angeles during this period. For more detailed information, consult the newspapers below (the numbers correspond to the organization):

(1) *La Estrella*, Jan. 25, 1855; (2) *El Clamor Público*, May 16, 1857; (3) *La Crónica*, June 10, 1872; (4) *La Crónica*, July 3, 1875; (5) *El Joven*, Sept. 18, 1877; (6) *Las Dos Repúblicas*, Nov. 11, 1893; (7) *El Joven*, Sept. 18, 1877; (8) *Las Dos Repúblicas*, Nov. 11, 1893; (9) *El Joven*, April 12, 1878; (10) *La Crónica*, May 19, 1883; (11) *The Young Republican*, Oct. 16, 1886, (12) *Las Dos Repúblicas*, July 22, 1893; (13) *Las Dos Repúblicas*, Aug. 26, 1896; (14) *Las Dos Repúblicas*, Jan. 30, 1897; (15) *Las Dos Re-públicas*, Jan. 30, 1897.

Mexican-American businessmen, offering low-cost medical and life insurance policies, and providing a vari-ety of social services needed by the community. La Sociedad was not the first mutualista in Los Angeles.

During the 1840's, a group of hacendados had formed Los Amigos del Pais with the dual purposes of providing pensions and stimulating the reading of liter-ature.[86] It had been disbanded during the Mexican War, and in 1875 La Sociedad began. Incorporated under state laws, La Sociedad proposed to construct a hospital for the poor and to raise capital for charitable purposes.

There were 11 Mexican-Americans on the board of directors, including José Carrillo and E. F. Teodoli.[87] La Sociedad met in Druid Hall on the Downey Block and occasionally held meetings in members' homes. To raise money for investment projects and the hospital, they sponsored concerts and dances. They also had wider interests in improving the quality of life in the community. In 1879 they submitted a petition to the Common Council proposing that a Spanish-language school be built. In 1894 they ran ads in *Las Dos Repúblicas* soliciting proposals for community development.[88]

These formal groups developed ethnic consciousness among the Spanish-speaking by giving organizational form to the life of the community. They sponsored social and political activities that developed the symbolic identification of La Raza as a separate cultural entity. The fact that these organizations were so numerous indicated a need within the community for new avenues of communication. They, along with the immigrant societies and newspapers, helped develop a new relational fabric, one that had not been present or even necessary in Mexican times. Out of their activities, the Spanish-speaking began to form a new personal identity that was more abstract and conceptual, linked to Mexico and Latin America by the cords of La Raza.

86. Bancroft, *History of California,* vol. 4, p. 629.

87. "Articles of Incorporation of Sociedad-Hispano Americana, December 9, 1875" (ms., L.A. Superior Court).

88. "La Sociedad Hispano-Americana de Beneficia Mutua to the Mayor and Common Council," October 2, 1879 (ms., Coronel Collection, L.A. Mus. Nat. Hist.); *Las Dos Repúblicas,* May 5, 1894.

CHAPTER FIVE

Isolation: Geographic, Political, Spiritual

The concept of the *barrio* is an ancient one, deriving from the blending of Spanish and pre-Columbian cultures. The Aztecs had developed a communal clan unit called the *calpulli*, which was a group of extended families related to each other by kinship and marriage. At the time of the Spanish conquest in 1519, the Aztec capital, Tenochtitlán, had more than 60 *calpullis*. [1] The Conquistadores called these family-oriented neighborhoods "barrios," since this word had the same approximate meaning in Spain. [2] Over time, the term "barrio" in Mexico came to refer to loosely defined sections of cities and pueblos. It was usually the place where the laboring classes lived.

The Spanish-speaking pioneers on New Spain's northern frontier used this term prior to the American conquest in 1848. Santa Fé, New Mexico, for example, had a barrio of Nahua-speaking Indians who had ac-

---

1. Also called *chinancalli* and *tlaxilacalli*. Family ties seem to have been the basis of the *calpulli* division, although the term was also used to describe groups of unrelated families that were political subdivisions of the Aztec tribute state. Not all *calpullis* were located in towns or cities. See Charles Gibson, *Los Aztecas bajo el domino español, 1519–1810*, p. 154.

2. The earliest recorded usage of the term "barrio"—meaning zone or dependency of the city—was in the eleventh century. The word may be from the Arabic *barr*, the Roman *barrium*, or the Catalan *barri*. See J. Caromonias, *Diccionario Crítico: Etimológico de la Lengua Castellana*, pp. 413–414.

companied Oñate's expedition of 1598. In addition, there seems to be evidence that many pueblos in both New Mexico and Northern Mexico had Indian barrios.[3] There is no evidence, as yet, that the term was used in California before 1848. But the place where the Yang-na Indians lived near Los Angeles before 1836 may have been considered a barrio.[4]

With the Anglo conquest, the term "barrio" took on a special meaning, signifying the region of the town where only the Spanish-speaking lived. In Los Angeles, Spanish-language editors began to write about the special problems of the barrio as early as 1872.[5] The Anglos called this place Sonora Town. For the Spanish-speaking, it was a place where they could feel at home and abandon the masks they wore in the Anglo world. While for many the barrio may have signified a place of familial warmth and brotherhood, it was also a place of poverty, crime, illness, and despair. To this day, many Chicanos continue to feel ambivalent about the barrio. The *comunidad* is the basis of a dynamic Chicano cultural upwelling, but it also continues to be a place of exploitation and poverty.[6]

The historical dynamics of the segregation of Mexican-Americans in the pueblo of Los Angeles are analyzed in this chapter. To what degree and at what rate did they become isolated from the Anglo-American population? What were some of the causes and consequences of their geographic and cultural segregation? The historical answers to these questions

3. Jack D. Forbes, *Aztecas del Norte: The Chicanos of Aztlán*, pp. 72–76.

4. Antonio Blanco does not list "barrio" as a word used in California prior to 1848. Blanco, *La Lengua Española en la Historia de California*.

5. See *La Crónica*, July 26, 1872; Feb. 10, 1875; May 16, 1877; Sept. 15, 1883.

6. This ambivalence is clear in a number of Chicano-movement writings; "The Plan of Santa Barbara," for example, states: "Man is never closer to himself than when he is close to his community," but "the barrio and the colonia remained exploited, impoverished, and marginal." Livie Isaura Duran and H. Russell Bernard, eds., *Introduction to Chicano Studies: A Reader*, pp. 533–535.

will enable us to better assess the dimensions of contemporary urban problems facing the Spanish-speaking in the Southwest.

Geographic Segregation

Prior to 1860, when the Mexican-American population was about three-fourths of the city's total, segregation was not geographical but social. The pueblo was divided into rich and poor areas (see Map 1). Most of the *pobres,* recent Mexican immigrants and laborers, lived in Sonora Town north of First Street.[7] The wealthy Californios who had town houses surrounding the plaza gradually abandoned them as the barrio expanded. By the 1860's, the plaza was a slum that included a Chinese ghetto called "Nigger Alley" by the Anglos. Here saloons and brothels flourished. Later, when the Southern Pacific and Los Angeles Independence Railroad began construction of their lines, Mexican and Mexican-American railroad workers also took up residence in the area north of the plaza.

In the 1860's, about half of the city's population was Spanish-surnamed, and Mexican-Americans began to be segregated in terms of property-holdings and land investments. In 1861 the bulk of Mexican-American property-owners were located in the core of the city, an area that corresponded to the heaviest population concentration of the old Mexican pueblo (see Map 2). The second most populous area, in terms of Mexican-American property ownership, was the southern section of the city. This had traditionally been a small farming region.

7. A NOTE ON MAPS: Map 1, showing Los Angeles in 1849, is traced from a copy of the well-known map drawn by Lieutenant E. O. C. Ord and William R. Hutton in 1849, and referred to as "Ord's Map of Los Angeles." A copy of this map is reproduced in William W. Robinson's *Maps of Los Angeles: From Ord's Survey of 1849 to the End of the Boom of the 80's.* This book contains an excellent discussion of the evolution of cartography in the city and contains several maps that are useful for studying geographical change. Maps 2 and 3 are traced from an original done by H. J. Stevenson in 1876 (in L.A. County Mus. Nat. Hist.).

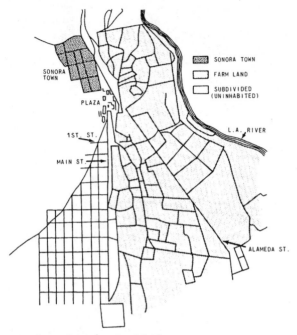

MAP I. *Los Angeles in 1849.*
Drawn from original map by E.O.C. Ord, August 29, 1849.

By the 1870's Mexican-Americans were a numerical minority. The existing patterns of property ownership evident in 1861 continued. During the 15 years between 1861 and 1876, Mexican-Americans increased their ownership of the core and southern localities. This was true both in terms of the absolute numbers of property-holders and in terms of the value of real estate owned (see Table 30).

Evidently what happened during the 'sixties was that many of the rich, who formerly had lived on ranches and farms in the southern section of the city, or in the county, had moved into the core area and bought property. Between 1861 and 1876, the rate of Mexican-American property improvement, in land and structures, increased within the core area more than in any other section of Mexican-American residence. In 1861 only two Mexican-Americans had owned property worth more than 2,000 dollars in the central region; by

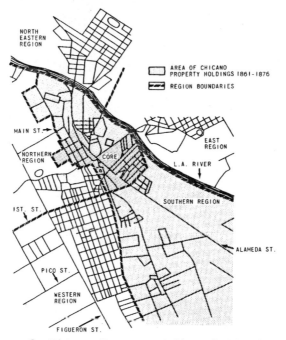

MAP 2. *Chicano Property-Holders, 1861–1876.*
Drawn from original map by H. J. Stevenson, 1876.

1876 more than 19 Spanish-surnamed landowners had moved in and bought property worth more than this amount.

During the 1870's the majority of Mexican-American property-holders continued to live in the central and southern sections of the city. In 1861 only 7 landholders—about 8 percent of the total number of owners—had parcels outside these areas. By 1876 this number had increased to 34, or about 17 percent of Mexican-American landholders. The geographic segregation of property-holders therefore did not change significantly.

Patterns of property ownership and investment were not entirely indicative of geographic concentration among the Spanish-speaking population. In order to get a better idea of the residence patterns of non-property-holders, it is necessary to refer to the 1880

TABLE 30
Mexican-American Property-Owners and Value of Holdings by Section of City, 1861–1876

Section	Number of property holders		Number owning property valued at:							
			$1–500		$501–2000		$2001–5000		Over $5000	
	1861	1876	1861	1876	1861	1876	1861	1876	1861	1876
Core	69	111	55	58	9	34	2	14	0	5
South	11	56	4	10	5	34	1	8	1	4
Northeast	2	7	0	5	1	0	0	1	1	1
West	4	18	2	8	2	6	0	4	0	0
East	1	9	1	4	0	2	0	1	0	2
Total	87	201	62	85	17	76	3	28	2	12

SOURCE: Computer analysis of assessment rolls: *Assessment Roll for the County of Los Angeles, City, 1861*, and *Assessment Book for the Property of Los Angeles County, City, 1876* (both in L.A. County Mus. Nat. Hist.).

census which listed street addresses. In general, the census confirms the notion that the bulk of Mexican-Americans continued to live in the southern and core sections of Los Angeles into the 1880's.

Table 31 shows that more than 70 percent of the Mexican-Americans lived in these two areas in 1880. While census-ward boundaries did not correspond exactly to the areas of heaviest property ownership, they were roughly analogous. Ward 1 roughly corresponded to the core area; Wards 2 and 4 incorporated most of the southern section. Nearly 49 percent of the total Mexican-American population lived in Ward 1; about 22 percent lived in Ward 2. In the core area, Mexican-Americans were in the majority; elsewhere they were a minority.

After 1880, Mexican-Americans were more segre-

TABLE 31

Spanish-Surnamed Population by Wards,
1880

	Ward 1	Ward 2	Ward 3	Ward 4	Ward 5
Percentage of Mexican-Americans to total population of ward	86.5	16.6	6.4	17.9	23.4
Percentage of all L.A. Mexican-Americans in ward	48.7	21.8	7.2	10.9	11.2
Total Mexican-American population in ward	1,072	481	159	240	248
Total population, both Anglo and Mexican-American, in ward	1,239	2,894	2,459	1,334	1,057

SOURCE: Computer analysis of 1880 census returns.

gated from the Anglo population. To measure the degree to which this was true, I have used the Index of Residential Dissimilarity (D), first developed by Otis Dudley Duncan and Beverly Duncan.[8] The measure has been used by a number of researchers to assess comparative segregation.[9]

The Index of Residential Dissimilarity varies from 0 (no segregation) to 100 (total segregation). In 1880 the Los Angeles Spanish-speaking had a D score of 36.9; by 1960 their D score had risen to 57.4. In terms of this index, they had become more segregated over the 80-year period. The Mexican-Americans in Los Angeles in 1880 were about as segregated as those Chicanos who, in 1960, lived in San Francisco (38.1), Laredo, Texas (39.4), or Galveston, Texas (33.4).[10]

This analysis of segregation, based upon census-ward figures, fails to accurately measure geographical segregation involving more than one ward. Ward boundaries were gerrymandered for the convenience of office-holders, and thus cut across areas of heavy Mexican-American residence.[11] In order to investigate the changing geographic boundaries of the barrio, it is

8. Otis Dudley Duncan and Beverly Duncan, "Residential Distribution and Occupational Stratification," *J. Sociol.*

The formula used to compute this Index is:

$$D = \left(\frac{N_{ij}}{T_j} - \frac{N_{jk}}{T_k} \right) /2$$

where D is the Index of Dissimilarity between two ethnic groups (in this case the Mexican-American and Anglo-American populations):

i = the particular subarea in the city;

N (ij) = the number of Mexican-Americans in area i;

N (jk) = the number of Anglo-Americans in area i;

T (j) = the total Mexican-American population in the city;

T (k) = the total Anglo-American population in the city.

9. Joan W. Moore and Frank G. Mittlebach, *Residential Segregation in the Urban Southwest*, p. B–1, Appendix B.

10. *Ibid.*, p. 16.

11. This problem, inherent in studying census tracts to determine segregation, has been discussed by Otis Dudley Duncan and Beverly Duncan, "Methodological Analysis of Segregation Indexes," *Am. Sociol. Rev.*, pp. 215–216.

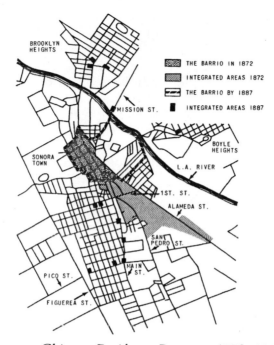

MAP 3. *Chicano Residence Patterns, 1872–1887.*
Drawn from original map by H. J. Stevenson, 1876.

necessary to plot the residences of the Spanish-
surnamed by blocks over a period of time.

This can be done using the Los Angeles city directories for 1872 and 1887–88.[12] The 1872 directory was
selected because it was the first city directory published
in the pueblo and the first document to list street addresses. More than 270 Mexican-American heads of
households were recorded. The 1887–88 directory
listed about 280 Mexican-American family heads and
their residences.

Map 3 shows the results of a plotting of street residences for Mexican-American families during the
period 1872–1888. In 1872 the heaviest concentration of
Mexican-Americans was north of the plaza and west of
Main Street. In this area stood residential dwellings,

12. *The First Los Angeles City and County Directory, 1872,* and
Los Angeles City Directory, 1887–1888.

mostly adobes. In the plaza area there was a mixture of detached residences, small businesses, and slums. Only a few Mexican-Americans lived east of the Los Angeles River; these families lived on Downey Street within the predominantly Anglo subdivision of Brooklyn Heights. South of the plaza, Mexican-American residences were more widely separated and integrated with their neighborhoods. Some families lived on small farms along Alameda, San Pedro, and Washington Streets, and others lived in small residences and shops located along Main Street.

Mexican-Americans were most segregated from the Anglo-American population in the area north of the plaza. Here they composed more than 80 percent of the population. In the rural areas, Mexican-American families maintained a degree of residential segregation by living in clusters. Segregation was least along south Main Street, where Mexican-American residences and shops were interspersed with those of the Anglos. Properly speaking, the barrio—as an ethnic enclave— was the ten-block area bounded by Short, Main, Yale, and College Streets.

A significant change in the shape of the barrio, as it evolved to 1887, was the result of the diffusion of a number of Spanish-surnamed families across the Los Angeles River into what is now East Los Angeles. By 1887 some families lived along Chestnut, Hansen, and Hawkins Streets in Brooklyn Heights and along Echandia Street in Boyle Heights. Mexican-Americans also lived along Mission Street on the east side of the river. Most of those who moved into East Los Angeles were skilled craftsmen or merchants in service occupations: saddlemakers, butchers, or gardeners. Living as they did, removed from the bulk of the Mexican-Americans, they were undoubtedly dependent on the Anglo population for their trade. A few families also moved into the Anglo suburbs southwest of Main and First Streets. Most of these new residences were the homes of professionals: druggists, engineers, and lawyers. They lived on Grand, Hill, and Olive Streets, which were at that time fashionable residential addresses. These marginal families, living outside the barrio by 1887–88, composed only about 12 percent of the total Mexican-American population listed in the city directory.

The more important trend was toward concentration and segregation. By 1887, the family clusters in the rural areas had disappeared and more Mexican-Americans were residing in the blocks east of Main and north of First Street. As a result, the barrio expanded so that relatively more Mexican-Americans were living in a segregated neighborhood. In 1872 about 52 percent of the families lived within a geographically definable barrio; by 1887, about 55 percent lived in the same barrio and in its recent additions.

Whether this increasing segregation was self-imposed or forced is difficult to say. It probably resulted from the convergence of several influences: the negative forces of poverty and transiency interacted with the positive forces of pride, language, and family solidarity.

During the period 1850–1880 the poorest section of the city, measured in terms of the rental and purchase of homes, was the core area. Here stood the oldest houses, most of them adobes pre-dating the American era. Rents were low, and small adobes might be purchased for as little as 100 dollars. In the newer tracts, developments east of the Los Angeles River and south of First Street, property values were higher. Since most of the newer houses were built of brick or wood, they were beyond the means of the average Mexican-American laborer.

Another factor accounting for the segregation of the Spanish-speaking in the core and southern sections was the marked transiency of the Mexican-American population. We have already noted that for the entire period 1844–1880 the persistence rate was less than 1 percent. The continued movement of the Mexican-American population into and out of the pueblo insured that the community would always be marginal.

Spanish-speaking immigrants from rural areas of California, the Southwest, or Mexico had to learn how to survive in the city. In this they had to depend heavily on the experiences of those Mexican-Americans who were already established. Knowing little if any English and being unaccustomed to city life, these immigrants found it easier to seek employment, housing, and companionship in the barrio. This conjecture is supported by the fact that in 1880 more than 83 percent of the Mexican immigrants to the city lived in the core and southern sections. [13]

Finally, whatever its implications for the socioeconomic fortunes of Mexican-Americans, the creation of the barrio was a positive accomplishment. The barrio gave a geographical identity, a feeling of being at home, to the dispossessed and poor. It was a place, a traditional place, that offered some security in the midst of the city's social and economic turmoil. We have already seen that a new ethnic pride was beginning to develop. The Spanish-speaking were creating a positive sense of community through their political associations and newspapers. This revitalization would have been impossible had the Spanish-speaking been diffused throughout the city. The creation of the barrio insured ethnic survival. Proximity of residence reinforced the language, religion, and social habits of the Mexican-Americans and thus insured the continuation of their distinctive culture.

Political Decline

During the 1870's and 1880's, the Spanish-speaking of Los Angeles became more and more segregated geographically. Politically, too, the Mexican-Americans were cut off from the larger society. In part the political decline of the Spanish-speaking was due to geographic segregation. As a voting bloc, Mexican-

13. A computer analysis of head of household's place of birth by wards in 1880 showed the following:

Place of Birth	Ward 1	Ward 2	Ward 3	Ward 4	Ward 5
Mexico	78	48	19	30	14
California	132	65	10	30	25
Other	10	4	1	0	0

American political strength was diluted by ward boundaries that split up the barrio. And almost 50 percent of the Spanish-speaking population lived outside the original barrio in the 1870's and 1880's—thus a segment of the population tended to lack the political concerns that moved those who continued to live in the core area. Furthermore, an affluent minority tended toward assimilation with the Anglo-Americans, further diluting the potential strength of the Mexican-American voting bloc.

The very nature of Mexican-American society also tended to diffuse ethnicity as a force for political unity. For, despite the violence and discrimination they endured, Mexican-Americans held their society remarkably open to Anglo participation. This openness, perhaps a continuation of an older tradition of tolerance, resulted in contingents of Anglos participating in almost all the Mexican-American clubs, political organizations, and newspapers. In 1875 James Hayes was elected to the founding board of La Sociedad Hispano-Americana; later John Kays was elected its secretary.[14] Dr. K. D. Wise and William Workman were involved in La Sociedad's project to build a hospital, and donated large sums of money.[15] William S. Ryan and L. Seamons were Anglo members of Corte Colon, an exclusive Spanish-speaking fraternity. C. M. Forester was vice-president of El Club Filharmonico Mexicano, and A. R. Roth was treasurer of La Junta Patriótica Mexicana.[16] Anglo-Americans also participated in the celebration of Mexican national holidays. In 1878 W. R. Betts, W. W. Moore, R. L. Blanchet, and F. C. Berry were listed as attendants for the Mexican Independence Day parade.[17] In 1883 C. J. Childs was

14. Los Angeles Superior Court, "Articles of Incorporation of La Sociedad Hispano-Americana, December 9, 1875" (ms.). See also *La Crónica,* May 12, 1877.

15. *La Crónica,* Feb. 7, 1877.

16. *Las Dos Repúblicas,* Nov. 11, 1893; Aug. 26, 1896; Sept. 15, 1897.

17. *La Crónica,* Sept. 18, 1878.

Grand Marshal for this occasion, and A. H. Howard and C. M. Young were among the speakers of the day.[18]

The Spanish-language press also showed evidence of Anglo participation. In the early years, during the 1850's, most of the regular subscribers to *El Clamor Público* were Anglos who read Spanish.[19] Anglo merchants and professionals were anxious to place ads in the Spanish-language newspapers, and at times the majority of the ads were printed in English. The Californio press, in particular, was often addressed to an interethnic audience. *La Crónica,* for example, expressed the hope that the paper would "serve as a vehicle of friendship, harmony, and understanding among our citizens, without exception of personalities or nationalities."[20]

Besides a willingness to welcome the Anglo-Americans into their political and social organizations, the Mexican-Americans were also anxious to participate in what they understood to be the benefits of the American system of government. Usually the upper classes led in attempts to smooth over cultural and racial differences and to pledge their allegiance to the American flag. In 1855 Francisco Ramirez took note of the 4th of July and called it "the most glorious day in this history of the United States."[21] In 1872, Ignacio Sepúlveda addressed an American Independence Day celebration in English. He spoke of the infinite gratitude of the Spanish-speaking population for the democratic system that had been bestowed on them through the American Revolution. He said: "We are the recipients of infinite gifts, we

18. *La Crónica,* Sept. 16, 1883.
19. Francisco Ramírez commented that "the foreigners (meaning the Anglo-Americans) have shown much more enthusiasm for subscribing to our paper than our own Californios." ORIGINAL SPANISH: " . . . los estranjeros han mostrado mucho mas ardor para subscrirse a nuestro periodico que los mismos Californios." *El Clamor Público,* June 19, 1855.
20. *La Crónica,* Oct. 26, 1878.
21. *El Clamor Público,* July 3, 1855.

the recipients of the fruits of the labors of our great patriots, in the midst of a universal prosperity, we unite today to pay tribute to their valor; to renew our adherence to the principles they proclaimed and to demonstrate by our happiness our infinite gratitude."[22]

During the 1850's, the older respectable Californio leaders continued to exercise considerable influence and power within the pueblo government. For the most part, they had the support of influential and wealthy Anglo-Americans like Abel Stearns and Juan Warner who were sympathetic to the Californio cause.

The Americans, along with their Californio allies, formed a political junta to select a slate of candidates to run in the first mayoral election after the conquest. Some of the older Californios, not used to such electoral procedures, believed the purpose of the meetings was to plot the overthrow of the existing military government. Said John Griffen, who attended one of the meetings of the junta: "Several of them [the Californios] asked me what it all means, and I have tried to explain it as well as I could see. The other night, at the junta at Don Abel's [Sterns], old Carrillo got up and wished to know what the devil they meant by calling him to such a treasonable meeting; what Col. Richard B. Mason [the military-appointed mayor] had done that they wished to kick him out of office . . . [and] that he would not countenance or support any such movements."[23] Eventually the Californios' confusion was dispelled, and the junta selected Stephen C. Foster, José Carmen del Lugo, and Juan Sepúlveda. They were all elected and served their terms that year.

When another junta met in 1849 to select representatives to the State Constitutional Convention, the same tendencies prevailed. The junta selected Hugo Reid, José A. Carrillo, Stephen Foster, Don Abel

22. Printed in English and Spanish in *La Crónica*, July 13, 1873.
23. Letter from John S. Griffen, M.D., to Col. J. D. Stevenson, March 11, 1849 (privately printed).

Stearns, and Manuel Dominguez to be the representatives from the southern districts.[24]

At the convention only 6 of the 73 delegates were Californios. These were José Carrillo and Manuel Dominguez from Los Angeles, Mariano Vallejo from Sonoma, Jacinto Rodriguez and Juan M. Covarrubias from San Luis Obispo, and Pablo de la Guerra from Santa Barbara.[25] Despite their small numbers, they influenced the debates over suffrage, community property, and the state boundaries.

De la Guerra led the Californio delegates in opposing the limitation of suffrage to white males, arguing that many Californios were not white and thus would be denied the franchise. Through his efforts and those of the other Californio delegates, the convention modified its proposal to include "white male citizens of Mexico" and tax-paying Indians.[26] The Californios, with some Anglo-American support, also persuaded the convention to retain Mexican community-property laws. Old Carrillo helped lead a move to keep southern and northern California within one state boundary.[27]

Throughout the nineteenth century, southern California was a Democratic Party stronghold. This was mainly due to the large Catholic population and the migration of Anglo Southerners into the region. Mexican-American citizens were lured into the party organization by the promise of local and state offices. In 1852 and again in 1853, Antonio F. Coronel was the chairman of the Los Angeles County Democratic Committee. Many other Californios also were active in the party organization in the 1850's. Table 32 lists them, along with their dates of involvement.

Since the Spanish-speaking population was the majority in the '50's, the Democratic Party had to tread lightly. By drawing Californio leaders into the party,

24. Dakin, *A Scotch Paisano*, p. xi.
25. Woodrow J. Hansen, *The Search for Authority in California*, pp. 98–99.
26. *Ibid.*, p. 122.
27. *Ibid.*, pp. 144, 172.

TABLE 32

Los Angeles Californio Members of Local and State
Democratic Committees and Conventions,
1850–1860

Name	Date of election
1. Antonio Coronel	1852–1853
2. Ignacio del Valle	1852
3. Manuel Requena	1852
4. Pío Pico	1856
5. Victoriano Guerrero	1856
6. Juan Rubio	1856
7. Hilario Ybarra	1856
8. Juan Sepúlveda	1856
9. Cristobal Aguilar	1856
10. Augustín Olvera	1856
11. Mariano Lugo	1856
12. Victoriano Lugo	1856
13. Juan Padilla	1858
14. Francisco Campo	1858
15. Ignacio Palomares	1858
16. Juan Ávila	1858

SOURCE: Various editions of local Californio newspapers,
1850–1860, primarily El Clamor Público, which listed the
members of the Los Angeles County Democratic Central
Committee on April 26, 1856; June 11, 1858; and July 3,
1858; also a broadside dated Oct. 26, 1852 (Del Valle Collection, L.A. County Mus. Nat. Hist.).

they could count on a heavy Democratic turnout, as the
Spanish-speaking continued to follow their traditional
leaders. These Californios, in return, were rewarded
with political offices. In the period 1850–1859 no fewer
than 38 Californio residents of Los Angeles were elected
or appointed to local and state offices. Table 33 lists
these Californio office-holders.

In 1856, their relationship with the Democratic Party
was put to a test when a sizable contingent of Californio leaders bolted and endorsed the Republican presi-
dential candidate, John C. Frémont. About 30 Califor-

TABLE 33

Californios from Los Angeles Elected or
Appointed to State or Local Offices, 1850–1859

Name	Office held	Date
1. Manuel Gárfias	County Treasurer	1850
2. Julian Chavez	Member of Common Council	1850
3. Ygnacio del Valle	County Recorder	1850
4. Francisco Figueroa	City Treasurer	1850
5. Augustín Olvera	County Judge	1850
6. Manuel Requena	Member of Common Council	1850
7. Antonio Coronel	City Assessor	1851
8. Ygnacio del Valle	Member of Common Council	1851
9. Tomás Sanchez	Member of Common Council	1851
10. Ygnacio Coronel	Member of Common Council	1851
11. Augustín Olvera	Member of Common Council	1851
12. Pablo de la Guerra	County Marshal	1852
13. Ygnacio del Valle	State Assemblyman	1852
14. Julian Chavez	County Supervisor	1852
15. Manuel Requena	County Supervisor	1852
16. Manuel Botello	Member of Common Council	1852
17. Antonio Coronel	Mayor	1853
18. Pío Pico	Member of Common Council	1853
19. Ygnacio Coronel	City Assessor	1853
20. Leonard Cota	County Supervisor	1853
21. Cristobal Aguilar	County Supervisor	1854
22. Juan Sepúlveda	County Supervisor	1854
23. Antonio Coronel	Member of Common Council	1854
24. Augustín Olvera	County Supervisor	1855
25. Antonio Coronel	Assessor	1855
26. Andrés Pico	Government Official	1855
27. Juan Sepúlveda	Assessor	1857
28. Tomás Sanchez	County Supervisor	1857
29. Manuel Coronel	City Assessor	1858
30. Andrés Pico	State Assemblyman	1858
31. Bernardo Guirado	County Supervisor	1858
32. Tomás Sanchez	Sheriff	1859
33. Antonio Coronel	Member of Common Council	1859
34. Ygnacio Coronel	Member of Common Council	1859
35. Manuel Requena	Member of Common Council	1859
36. Gerónimo Ibarra	Member of Common Council	1859
37. Antonio Coronel	County Supervisor	1860
38. Andrés Pico	State Senator	1860

SOURCE: Various editions of the Californio press, primarily
La Estrella and *El Clamor Público*.

nios, led by the editor Francisco Ramírez, signed and published a petition supporting the Republican platform in *El Clamor Público,* October 4, 1856.

They argued that the Democratic candidates, Franklin Pierce and James Buchanan, were anti-Mexican. Pierce had supported filibustering expeditions into Nicaragua and advocated an American takeover of Cuba, expressing sentiments of Manifest Destiny. During the Mexican War, Buchanan had compared the Mexicans to Negro slaves. He said that "the Mexican nation is composed of Spaniards, Indians, and Negroes in all varieties, so that they can receive our slaves on perfectly equal grounds."[28] The Democrats, in turn, attempted to discredit the charge that their candidates were anti-Mexican by pointing out that Frémont, the opposition candidate, had personally been involved in immoralities, corruption, and murder during the Mexican War. Some Californios may have been persuaded that Frémont had ordered the murders of de Haro and Berryesa. But petitions and endorsements by other Californios in support of Frémont, as well as increasing racial bitterness in local elections, tended to push the Mexican-American vote toward the Republicans.[29]

Two incidents made Mexican-Americans aware of how the local Anglos regarded the participation of the Spanish-speaking in politics. When Antonio Coronel, former mayor of the pueblo and a loyal Democrat, ran for office in 1856, a group of Anglo Democrats assembled near the polling booths shouting: "Here comes another Greaser vote! Here comes another vote for the Negro! If Coronel, the Negro, comes to vote, stop him!"[30] Fears that the Democrats were prepared to deal with the Spanish-speaking as they dealt with their slaves seemed well-founded.

Prior to the national elections, local Democrats tried to split Los Angeles county into two districts in order

28. *El Clamor Público,* Nov. 1, 1856. See also Pitt, *Decline,* p. 199.

29. *Ibid.,* p. 200.

30. *El Clamor Público,* Oct. 4, 1856.

to increase Anglo control of city elections.[31] At the end of the year, Frémont, Coronel, and the proposed division all lost. But the ethnic antipathies they generated remained an undercurrent until after the Civil War. In 1859, when a group of former Frémont supporters again tried to challenge the Anglo-dominated Democratic Party by forming a "People's Slate," they were uniformly defeated. Local politics thereafter remained in the control of conservative Democrats.[32]

These revolts did little to enhance the political influence of those Californios who remained loyal to the party. Besides splitting the Spanish-speaking vote, the revolts cast doubt on the loyalty of the Californios. Consequently, the number of Mexican-Americans holding office diminished after 1860. But there were further reasons for this decline. After 1860, the Spanish-speaking vote was not crucial to getting elected: Mexican-Americans were fast becoming a numerical minority. Economic disasters also began to take a toll among the formerly wealthy Californio leaders. Accordingly, between 1860 and 1882, only one Californio, Manuel Domínguez, served on the Los Angeles County Democratic Central Committee. The political decline stabilized during the 1860's and there was little change in the pattern of Mexican-American office-holding during the next 20 years (see Table 34).

Throughout the decades following the war with Mexico, the Spanish-speaking held most of their political strength in the County of Los Angeles, not in the City. More than 50 percent of all Mexican-American office-holders in the period 1850–1880 won their elections or appointments in the county. But after 1859 Californio political strength, even in the outlying regions, declined to about half of what it had been earlier. Within city government there was a similar trend of decline and stabilization of political representation. The

31. Pitt, *Decline,* p. 201.
32. *Los Angeles Star,* Sept. 27 and Nov. 1, 15, and 22, 1859; also Pitt, *Decline,* p. 200.

TABLE 34

Los Angeles Mexican-American Office-Holders
by Level of Office,
1850–1879

Level of office	1850–1859	1860–1869	1870–1879
State-elected	4	3	2
State-appointed	0	0	2
County-elected	27	17	16
County-appointed	5	3	2
City-elected	20	6	9
City-appointed	1	2	0
Totals	57	31	31

SOURCE: A computer analysis of Mexican-American office-holders drawn from newspapers and secondary works, James M. Guinn, *A History of California and Environs*, vol. 1; Thomas H. Thompson, Augustus West, and J. Albert Wilson, *History of Los Angeles County, California, with Illustrations;* Charles W. Palm and Edward N. Buck (eds.), *Political Statistician.*

number of elected and appointed officials of Spanish surname decreased by more than half after 1860 and remained at a depressed level thereafter.

The fact that in the 20 years following 1860 there was no significant change in the total number of Los Angeles Mexican-Americans holding elected office challenges the general view expressed by other historians that the Spanish-speaking experienced a continuous linear decline in political influence. This was simply not the case in the city of Los Angeles. The real decline in political representation came after 1880 and was due, in part, to the loss of numerical strength as Anglo-American immigration increased.

At the same time, a high degree of Mexican-American geographic mobility created an unstable electorate for Spanish-speaking office-seekers. Without a permanent community of Spanish-speaking American citizens, the Californio politicians had to rely on Anglo-Americans for their electoral majorities. This was the case in 1869 when Ygnacio Sepúlveda defeated

C. E. Thompson for the office of county judge. The vote was 1,028 for Sepúlveda and 833 for Thompson. Anglo votes carried the day, since less than 450 male Mexican-Americans were of voting age and probably fewer than that number voted. The same Anglo-American support was evident in the 1882 election of Antonio Sepúlveda over B. W. Torwater for the office of auditor. In this election Sepúlveda garnered 3,784 votes to Torwater's 3,246. In 1880 the number of Mexican-Americans eligible to vote was fewer than 400.[33]

Californio politicians were successful in winning only those elections where they had, by family background or friendships, proved their assimilation into American society. By and large they were rich men whose interests ran parallel to those of the wealthiest and most respected Anglo-Americans. Table 35 shows a sample of 24 Mexican-American politicians with their socioeconomic backgrounds. Most were Californio ranchers, farmers, or merchants who held considerable property. As a group, these men were far removed from the mass of the Spanish-speaking, particularly the newly arrived Mexican immigrant or transient laborer.

Not surprisingly, there is no evidence of any effort on their part to ameliorate the pressing social and economic ills that plagued the barrio. The same family names continued to appear year after year for election on the Democratic ticket. There were very few new entrants into political life. Scions of the older families, who had proved their loyalty to the Anglo majority, continued to monopolize electoral politics for the Mexican-Americans. Although superficially the Spanish-speaking did not appear to lack political representation, in fact they did. For practical purposes, the mass of laborers in the barrio remained politically inarticulate and unrepresented.

33. Charles W. Palm and Edward N. Buck (eds.), *Political Statistician*, pp. 43–45. Figures of males of voting age are based on the 1870 and 1880 census counts.

Religious Segregation

The progressive isolation of Mexican-Americans, geographically and politically, was an indication that they were losing their power to influence the social environment. This growing social impotence extended into matters of religion as well. Mexican-Americans in the postwar decades became increasingly alienated from the institutional Church. Almost all of the priests and prelates within the Catholic Church of Los Angeles, after 1850, were either Spanish, French, or Italian. While most of them spoke Spanish, they were much more identified with the Californio upper class and with American Catholics than they were with the more numerous Mexican-born and native working class.

The last regularly appointed Mexican priest in the city was Father Gonzales Rubio, the confessor and secretary to the last Mexican bishop of California, The Right Reverend Francisco Diego y Moreno. In 1850, Bishop Moreno was replaced by a Spaniard, The Right Reverend Joseph Sadoc Alemany. Alemany removed Father Rubio and appointed Reverend Ancilutus Lestrade, a Frenchman, as priest in charge of the plaza church. For the next 25 years, the Spanish bishops and their European-born appointees ran the church and regulated the spiritual life of the Spanish-speaking. When The Right Reverend Taddeus Amat succeeded Bishop Alemany in 1854 and moved the episcopal residence from Santa Barbara to Los Angeles, he appointed Father Bernardo Raho, an Italian, as the new pastor of Nuestra Señora de Los Angeles. Father Raho died in 1862 and Bishop Amat's successor, The Right Reverend Francisco Mora, appointed Father Peter Verdaguer, a Frenchman, who served as pastor until the 1890's.[34]

34. The main outlines of ecclesiastical history for the city of Los Angeles in the nineteenth century can be drawn from the following works, all by Rev. Francis J. Weber: *Catholic Footprints in California; Rt. Rev. Joseph Sadoc Alemany, O.P., Bishop of Monterey; A Bio-*

TABLE 35
Social Characteristics of Los Angeles Mexican-American Political Leaders, 1850–1880

Name	Office held	Value of property held	Place of birth	Occupation
Cristobal Aguilar	Mayor	$ 1,800	Calif.	politician
Martín Aguirre	Sheriff	—	Calif.	farmer
Dionisio Bitiller	Assessor	5,000	Calif.	farmer
José Carrillo	Marshal	—	Calif.	rancher
Julian Chavez	County superintendent	1,250	N.M.	rancher
Antonio Coronel	Mayor	8,000	Mexico	merchant
Mariano Coronel	State senator	22,000	Mexico	farmer
Leonardo Cota	Sheriff	25,000	Calif.	politician
Manuel Dominguez	Delegate to Democratic Central Committee	—	Calif.	rancher
Francisco Figueroa	City treasurer	15,000	Mexico	merchant

Name	Office	Wealth	Birthplace	Occupation
Manuel Gárfias	County treasurer	7,000	Mexico	agriculturalist
Ylario Ybarra	Delegate to Democratic Central Committee	3,000	Calif.	farmer
José Lopez	Constable	750	Calif.	farmer
Francisco Ocampo	Rep. to County Democratic Committee	30,000	Mexico	rancher
Ygnacio Palomares	Rep. to County Democratic Committee	—	Calif.	rancher
Juan Ramirez	County evaluator	4,500	Calif.	vintner
Manuel Requena	County superintendent	23,000	Mexico	merchant
Antonio Rocha	City assessor	600	Calif.	farmer
José Rubio	Rep. to County Democratic Committee	1,500	Calif.	farmer
Tomás Sanchez	Sheriff	7,000	Calif.	grazier
José Sepúlveda	County superintendent	6,000	Calif.	rancher
Ramón Sotello	Auditor	—	Calif.	clerk
Julian Valdez	City councilman	—	Calif.	merchant
Reginaldo del Valle	State assemblyman	65,000	Calif.	lawyer

SOURCE: Manuscript census returns, 1850–1880, in combination with lists of political officials found in Californio newspapers.

During this period, the Catholic hierarchy was anxious to put into effect a program to Americanize the Church. In 1852 a Plenary Council of Bishops, meeting in Baltimore, Maryland, initiated a master plan that called for stricter enforcement of the tithe and an increase in parochial education. At the same time, the Council hoped to solidify the Church's control over Spanish-speaking Catholics in the Southwest by rebuilding the missions and regaining the Pious Fund, an investment fund that the Mexican government had expropriated during the secularization of the missions.[35]

In California there were occasional conflicts between Church officials and the Californios, especially when it came to collecting the tithe. But the vast majority of the *ricos* supported the new Church policies. When Bishop Amat decided to move his headquarters to the pueblo in 1858, a group of hacendados led by Manuel Requena, Ygnacio del Valle, Augustín Olvera, Antonio Coronel, and Julian Chavez raised funds to build his episcopal residence.[36] In 1855 this same hacendado elite lent its financial and moral support to bring the Sisters of Charity, a Baltimore-based order of nuns, to the pueblo. The upper class was prominent in all the major Church celebrations. When the plaza church was rebuilt in order to make it more suitable for Bishop Amat, Ygnacio del Valle and José Sepúlveda, along with Abel Stearns and Juan Sansevain, acted as godfathers during the consecration ceremonies.[37]

---

graphical Sketch of Rt. Rev. Francisco García y Moreno, the First Bishop of the Californias, 1775–1846; California's Reluctant Prelate: The Life and Times of Rt. Rev. Thaddeus Amat, C.M., 1811–1878; and Francisco Mora, Last of the Catalans. See also John Bernard McGloin, California's First Archhishop: The Life of Joseph Sadoc Alemany, O.P.; Gerald Geary, The Transfer of Ecclesiastical Jurisdiction in California, 1840–1853; and Edwin Hogue, "A History of Religion in Southern California" (Ph.D. diss.).

35. U.S. Dept. of State, The United States vs. Mexico in the Matter of the Case of the Pious Fund of the Californias, Appendix II. See also Pitt, Decline, p. 216.

36. El Clamor Público, Dec. 26, 1857.

37. Ibid., Dec. 27, 1856.

13. Antonio Coronel, one of the few Mexicanos elected mayor of Los Angeles after 1850. Courtesy of the Southwest Museum, Los Angeles.

14. The pueblo church, Nuestra Señora la Reina de Los Angeles, east of the plaza in 1875. Notice how the church's architecture has been changed by Anglo-American influence. Courtesy of the Huntington Library.

All of this, of course, was no change from the Mexican era when the Church had been the main bulwark of the upper classes. The continued alliance of the Church and the wealthy was a natural one, since the Church supported order, authority, and law. The pastoral letters of the Bishops, which were read in Spanish to the plaza faithful, emphasized the Church's controlling and moderating functions. In 1873, Bishop Amat told the congregation that the Church was "the main support of society and order, which imperatively demands the respect for legitimate authority and subjugation to legitimate laws."[38]

But even while the upper levels of the Church hierarchy were firmly in the hands of wealthy non-Mexicans, there was a kind of religious underground among Mexican-Americans. Fiestas, celebrating religious and secular holidays, were sometimes held without the sanctions of the Church or the *ricos*. In 1851, some Californios and American landholders voiced opposition to the proliferation of religious processions within the pueblo. The Church responded by withdrawing its sponsorship of the annual fiesta celebrating the anniversary of the founding of the city. The pobladores held the fiesta anyway. A northern California paper, *The Pacific*, remarked: "The anniversary of Our Lady Queen of Angels has been celebrated today with some pomp, although the priests declined sanctioning the usual procession. The reason given was that the local newspaper *(The Star)* had criticized the processions."[39]

Since these unofficial fiestas challenged their traditional social leadership, the *gente de razón* occasionally opposed them. In 1874, *La Crónica's* editors were "opposed to the multiplication of these fiestas and days of diversion."[40] Nevertheless, a number of quasi-religious

38. Hogue, "History of Religion," p. 296.
39. *The Pacific*, Sept. 26, 1851; Hogue, "History of Religion," p. 67.
40. *La Crónica*, May 5, 1874.

celebrations continued to be held without the official benediction of either the Church or the upper classes. On San Juan Day, June 24th, some of the town's Indians and Mestizos gathered beside the Los Angeles River at dawn to bathe themselves. It was believed that if they bathed in running water on this day, their health would be insured for the rest of the year. Many families also continued to hold their own religious ceremonies. Late in the evening, led by the head of the family, they would gather to pray for lost souls in purgatory. This was called La Adoración de los Animos en Purgatorio.[41]

For many Mexican-Americans, *curanderos*—spiritual healers—continued to have religious authority. In the Mexican era, Indian shamanic lore had mixed with Catholicism to produce a complex medicinal art that involved the control of both the spiritual and physical worlds. Curanderos used herbs and incantations to dispel evil spirits and physical ills. In 1850, Narciso Botello traveled to the curandera Josefa Romero in San José. Doctors had been unable to help Botello, but the curandera, using "yerbas de pais" or local herbs, completely cured him.[42] In 1856 Francisco Rodriguez, another Los Angeles resident, borrowed 20 dollars from Abel Stearns to pay for a curandera to treat his wife.[43] All of this, of course, was contrary to the teachings of the Church. Thus, as mystic healers, the curanderos provided Mexican-Americans with an alternative source of spiritual authority.[44]

In any case, for most Mexican-Americans, the Church's symbolic and spiritual meanings were more important than its hierarchy. The most important rites of passage—baptism, marriage, and burial—were al-

41. Packman, *Leather Dollars,* pp. 27–28.
42. Narciso Botello, *Anales del Sur de la California,* Jan. 27, 1878 (ms., Bancroft Library).
43. Francisco Rodriguez to Abel Stearns, Oct. 27, 1856 (ms., Stearns Collection, Huntington Library).
44. See Griswold del Castillo, "Health and the Mexican-Americans in Los Angeles, 1850–1887," *J. Mex.-Am. Hist.*

ways of special significance to the Mexican-American. Even if he never attended a mass, he felt these sacraments to be as essential as life itself.

The strength of this feeling was illustrated by an incident that took place in 1854 when a local priest, probably Father Lestrade, refused to bury a Mexican woman because she had died in sin. One night, 40 of her friends, mostly Mexican immigrants, stole into the churchyard and buried her in a lay ceremony. The Anglo-American Catholic community was horrified at this pagan practice, called them a "mutinous rabble" and attacked the deed as an example of the uncivilized habits of Spanish-speaking people in general. This episode, coming as it did during a period of racial tension in the pueblo, provoked the upper class Californios to form a united front in order to pacify Anglo critics. The next day they banished the Mexicans who had committed the deed.[45]

The main change from Mexican times regarding the Catholic religion was that the Spanish-speaking became more isolated from the institutional Church. Mexican-Americans did not cease calling themselves Catholics, but their allegiances to what was becoming an alien institution grew more tenuous and informal. Thus when the editors of *Las Dos Repúblicas* lauded Mexican-Americans for "having conserved their ancient beliefs," they had in mind a communality of faith, not practice.[46] Loyalty to the Church could not be gauged by attendance at Mass. Indeed, fewer and fewer pobladores went to formal worship services.[47]

In 1876, this isolation from the church became geographic as well as spiritual. In that year Bishop Amat finished building St. Viviana's Cathedral, the city's second Catholic church. It soon became the exclusive place of worship for the Anglo population. The plaza church became a segregated church for the Spanish-

45. Pitt, *Decline,* p. 221.
46. *Las Dos Repúblicas,* April 2, 1893.
47. Pitt, *Decline,* p. 215.

speaking.[48] Despite their isolation and fall from promi-
nence, Mexican-Americans took a special pride in their
little church on the plaza. An anonymous letter writer
in 1893 found it "infinitely more bright and beautiful"
than the new Cathedral.[49] With the construction of
other predominantly Anglo churches, St. Vincent's and
St. Andrew's in 1886, Sacred Heart in 1887, and St.
Joseph's in 1888, the plaza church fell into official in-
significance.[50] By the 1880's the spiritual segregation
into rich and poor, so evident in earlier years, was
finally confirmed by geographic fact.

48. Hogue, "History of Religon," p. 302.
49. *Las Dos Repúblicas,* April 21, 1893.
50. For a list of church construction in the nineteenth century, I
am indebted to Mrs. Maime Sinclair, secretary to the Archdiocese
of Los Angeles.

CONCLUSION

As a result of forces set in motion by the Anglo-American conquest and the Gold Rush, the Mexican pobladores of Los Angeles began a forced march into the twentieth century. Their destination was fixed by accelerating commercial and technological change. To guide them during these years of transition, the Spanish-speaking instinctively turned to a cultural map they had developed throughout their earlier history. The Indian, the Spaniard, and the Mexican had given the traditions that were to direct them in the new era. But these old ways proved to be increasingly unreliable in traveling the strange paths laid down for them by their conquerors. Defeated and confused, they grappled with a new social order, haunted by the world they had known as children.

In the 1890's multiple suicide became a topic of discussion in the town's only Spanish-language newspaper. "The cause of so much suicide," said the editor of *Las Dos Repúblicas* on March 26, 1893, "is the lack of a sane education, much misery, huge ambitions, a lot of fanaticism, and little true faith." After 50 years of Anglo-American rule, the older Californio culture, with its ability to bind together and give meaning to everyday life, had lost its vitality. In its place grew a new ethnic culture, one better adapted to the changed environment (see Table 36).

In dress and manner, the Mexican-American population of the city now resembled their Anglo neighbors more than their Mexican cousins. Wealthy Californios built Victorian mansions and organized literary clubs. Mexican-American laborers wore blue denim work clothes and rode the streetcar to work. Rural immigrants from Mexico found some things familiar: the adobe buildings that continued to serve as houses for most of the population, the dances and serenades that echoed each night, the familiar foods sold in the shops on Main Street. But they must have been bewildered by so much that was different. Many Mexican-Americans Anglicized their names and spoke a new dialect of Spanish containing words borrowed from English. Barrio gossip must have been strange to the immigrants as well as to the older Californios. Children with names like Gutierrez and Coronel understood their Spanish-speaking grandparents and parents, but usually answered them in English which both understood. Barrio newspapers printed many articles in English and were financed by ads from Anglo merchants.

The details of this transmutation from a Mexican pueblo to a Mexican-American barrio has been examined in the preceding chapters. Economically, Mexican-Americans were progressively excluded from the growth of the city. La Raza suffered a decline in property holdings. The number of Mexican-Americans who were able to find new jobs decreased. The traditional rancho economy was broken and buried under new laws, exorbitant legal fees, taxes, and violence. Fewer and fewer Mexican-Americans found Los Angeles a hospitable place to raise their families, and they left in large numbers. By 1880, less than one family in ten could say that they had lived in the pueblo since the beginning of the American regime.

There were some exceptions to this trend of economic decline and flight. After 1870 more Spanish-speaking people were able to hold on to small parcels of land than could in earlier decades. Despite the high transiency rate, those who continued to live in the pueblo were able to increase their property holdings to some small extent. The occupational distribution of the Mexican era remained unchanged except for slight improvements in the distribution of nonlaboring occupations. Small numbers of Mexican-Americans entered professional and skilled jobs, and the percentage who worked as manual laborers decreased slightly from what it had been in 1844.

But those who prospered were minor exceptions. Struggle and decline were the dominant pattern of the economic life for most Mexican-Americans in Los Angeles. But it would be wrong to conclude that they were completely submerged—economic oppression was the substratum out of which the pobladores forged new social and cultural patterns of survival within the family and community.

Changes in the size and composition of the family indicated something of the rate of modernization. The traditional extended family gave way to more fluid arrangements. Increasing numbers of women entered into common-law unions, intermarried with Anglo-Americans, found themselves as sole heads of households, became wage-earners, and received a formal education. Women married later and had fewer children. By 1880 the nuclear family dominated the domestic arrangements of the Spanish-speaking. The family and the Church ceased to be the main institutions for the socialization of La Raza. Many Mexican-Americans sent their children to English-language public schools to study new secular subjects. More and more Mexican-Americans learned to read and write, due less to public instruction than to increased Mexican immigration and private schooling.

New forms of social and cultural organization emerged to give direction to the ethnic society. Many Spanish-language newspapers and political and social clubs sprang up, giving the barrio a life apart from Anglo-American society. The web of activities, issues, conflicts, and sentiments sustained by the press and the organizations gave meaning to a community wracked by chaotic and violent events. Newspaper editors protested lynchings, robbery of lands, and less violent forms of discrimination. In the cantinas and on the street corners the pobladores celebrated in song and legend the deeds of quasi-revolutionary bandidos while other citizens organized celebrations of patriotic holidays. These were all signs that a new ethnic awareness and a new urban culture were being born.

The barrio was the matrix, the place where these new social realities found life and expression. By the 'eighties the Spanish-speaking population lived, for the most part, within a well defined adobe enclave surrounded by wood-framed Anglo-American suburbs. To the Anglos the barrio seemed to be a sleepy Mexican village, quaintly placed in the middle of their booming frontier city. They did not see that it was partially the creation of their own economic and social prejudice. Unable to advance economically, the mass of Mexican-Americans simply could not afford to move into the newer regions of the city. The barrio was the place where newly arrived Mexican immigrants could settle, if only for a short time, finding menial jobs, cheap housing, and temporary companionship, before they moved on to other barrios or colonias.

Despite increasing isolation, most of La Raza was anxious to participate in the larger society. The tragedy was that, except for a few Californios, most Anglos regarded them as Mexicans, a foreign group destined to disappear as had the Indians. Until then their poverty and segregation was justified by their refusal to speak or act like "Americans." A few Mexican-Americans were successful in meeting the new requirements—but the masses, forever stigmatized as a people of color, remained an alien group.

And so it was that the Spanish-speaking people of Los Angeles engaged the forces of industrialization, urbanization, and segregation. Later in the twentieth century, hundreds of thousands of Mexican immigrants, fleeing the Revolution of 1910, or lured to the United States by promises of jobs and a better life, invaded the old barrio, expanded its borders, and crossed the river to create present-day East Los Angeles.

An overview of this new barrio in 1970 shows an unexpected continuity of social patterns first developed

TABLE 36
Social Statistics for Los Angeles Chicanos,
1880 and 1970

Social characteristic	1880	1970
Mean family size	3.69	4.25
Mean number of children under 18 years of age	3.03	2.71
Percentage of female heads of household	29%	20%
Percentage of females in Chicano work force	12.2%	36.5%
Percentage of Chicano population born in Mexico	19.6%	24%
Percentage of school-age children enrolled	38%	53%
Percentage geographically mobile:		
1860–1880	90%	
1965–1970		57%
Percentage of work force[a] in:		
Ranching and farming	9%	0%
Professional	4	4
Mercantile	7	19
Skilled labor	15	31
Unskilled labor	65	46

SOURCE: Computer analysis of 1880 manuscript census returns. 1970 census data from U.S. Dept. of Commerce, Bureau of the Census, Social and Economic Statistics Administration, *General Social and Economic Statistics, California.*

a. 1970 census categories were included under 1880 categories 1–5:
  (1) Ranching and farming
      Farmers and farm managers
  (2) Professional
      Professional, technical, and kindred workers
  (3) Mercantile
      Managers and administrators (except farm sales workers)
      Clerical and kindred workers
  (4) Skilled labor
      Craftsmen, foremen, and kindred workers
      Transport and equipment operatives
      Service workers, except private household
  (5) Unskilled labor
      Operatives, except transport
      Laborers, farm laborers, and farm foremen
      Private household workers

in the nineteenth century. Now, as then, the vast majority of Chicanos live segregated from Anglo-Americans and are without meaningful political or religious representation. Most still work as laborers, skilled and unskilled. Mexican immigrants still compose about one-fourth of the population. The average size of families and the average numbers of children remain the same. The proportion of heads of households who are women has not changed dramatically. Ethnic newspapers and secondary organizations continue to be vehicles for community self-expression and identification. The contemporary Chicano movement, with its emphasis on racial pride and unity, appears to be an outgrowth of themes first articulated in past decades. Many basic societal and cultural tendencies of the present Chicano community have a direct relationship to the nineteenth-century history of the Sonora Town barrio.

The Censuses

1. Census Sources Used in Tables

1844: Marie E. Northrup, comp. "The Los Angeles Padrón of 1844." *Quarterly of the Historical Society of Southern California* 42, no. 4 (December 1960): 360–422.

1850: Maurice H. Newmark and Marco R. Newmark, eds. *The Census of Los Angeles, 1850.* Los Angeles: Times-Mirror Press, 1929.

1860: *Population Schedules of the Eighth Census of the United States, 1860.* Microfilm No. 653, Roll 59. Washington, D.C.: National Archives, 1965.

1870: *Population Schedules of the Ninth Census of the United States, 1870.* Microfilm No. 593, Roll 73. Washington, D.C.: National Archives, 1965.

1880: *Population Schedules of the Tenth Census of the United States, 1880.* Microfilm No. 102, Roll T9–67. Washington, D.C.: National Archives, 1967.

2. Discussion of Methods and Procedures

The United States manuscript census schedules contain a wealth of information. They have been little used by traditional historians; increasingly, historians influenced by the New Urban History are finding them a valuable resource. Many of the problems I encountered in using census documents were by no means unique to them alone. Compared with other handwritten nineteenth-century documents, such as the tax lists, birth and death records, and church documents, the census schedules are of high quality and remarkably consistent. Nevertheless, the information they contain is as problematic as life itself and should be interpreted with caution.

The first problem I had in preparing the statistical portions of this book was in transcribing the census data into computer-readable form. Luckily, both the 1844 and 1850 censuses had already been printed, so that all that remained was to keypunch the data. For the other documents the major problem was legibility. The handwriting of the various census-takers differed greatly. Legibility was important in deciphering the first and last names and places of birth in order to trace individuals through time and to determine their ethnic-group membership. To some extent this difficulty was minimized by enlarging the original manuscript census forms and having them printed on large paper. Still some names remained indecipherable.

Coding and keypunching were laborious and time-consuming, but not particularly difficult. Eventually I managed to keypunch the entire manuscript census returns for those whom I had classified as Mexican-Americans for each census year up to 1880. This involved over 10,000 cards, each containing 12 categories of information: residence number, last name, first name, age, sex, occupation, occupational code, place of birth, literacy, school attendance, race, and census year. Once processed for keypunching errors, the cards were used to make a magnetic tape that was then processed by several PL/1 programs. This data, along with a description of its format, is available at the Inter-University Consortium for Political Research, Ann Arbor, Michigan.

3. Statistical Errors in the Census

The most common error in the manuscript censuses was the incorrect spellings of Spanish first and last names. Few, if any, of the census-takers spoke Spanish, and their phonetic interpretation of Spanish surnames produced a number of variant spellings. Thus "Gonzales" became "Gonsales" or "Consalez"; "Chavez" became "Chaves" or "Chabes"; "Villa" became "Billa" or "Bila," and so on. That these errors in spelling were not more widespread is to the credit of the census-takers. Indeed, most of the names were spelled correctly.

There were other errors in the reportage of ages. Demographers believe that large-scale statistical surveys will always contain errors in age reporting. This is due to faulty memory and outright lying; although in the case of the Spanish-speaking, the language may have affected age reporting as well. There is always a tendency toward overreporting even-numbered ages and those ending in zeros and fives. The ages given for the very young and the elderly are most likely to contain errors.

In general, the language barriers between the census-takers, and the Spanish-speaking population increased the probability of error in reporting other census information. The difficult political and economic situation probably caused some Mexican-Americans to be suspicious of the motives of the census enumerators and to fabricate answers or avoid being counted. Unfortunately we cannot objectively measure the statistical effect of these fears and lack of communication on the accuracy of the census.

4. The 1850 and 1852 California Censuses

The 1850 federal census, conducted at the height of the Gold Rush, was at the time regarded as imperfectly taken. The crucial issue was political representation in both the national and state legislatures. The returns for three counties—San Francisco, Contra Costa, and Santa Clara—were lost before they reached Washington, D.C. As a consequence, Congress authorized the state to conduct its own census two years later.

With regard to the Spanish-speaking population of Los Angeles, it appears that the second census was no more accurate than the first. Governor Bigler admitted this to the State Legislature upon completion of the state census. It is difficult to compare these two censuses. The state census did not separate city and county residents as did the federal. The state census counted all Indians, while the federal counted only tax-paying Indians. The state census did not list literacy, school attendance, or property ownership as had the federal census. The 1852 census listed the citizenship status and state of residence before coming to California; the 1850 federal census lacked these categories.

It appeared to me that the 1852 census contained many more errors in the spelling of Spanish surnames than had the federal census of 1850. Names which were correctly spelled in 1850 were misspelled in 1852.

In 1852, they counted 913 more white persons living in Los Angeles County than had the federal census two years earlier. This has led some to conclude that the 1852 census was more complete than its predecessor. It seems much more likely that population differences between the two censuses were largely due to the Gold Rush migrations. It is entirely possible that 913 more white residents migrated into the county during the intercensus years.

Consequently, I have selected the 1850 federal census for study, rather than the state census. The federal document contains information on property ownership, literacy, and family composition which is lacking in the state documents.

5. Problems in Classifying Mexican-Americans in the Census

The federal government has had a good deal of trouble in classifying Mexican-Americans. As an ethnic group, Chicanos today do not have the status of a race, as do Blacks and Orientals. Yet in the past, they were regarded as a separate race. The 1930 census did have a category for those of the "Mexican race," but this was dropped in 1940. In 1950 and 1960 the census described the Chicano population as "white persons of Spanish surname." In 1970 many different criteria were used, including language, place of birth, and self-definition. But this more complicated procedure was carried out on only one-fifth of the country's population and did not really measure the entire Spanish-speaking community.

For this study the following criteria were used to select individuals from the censuses and classify them as members of the Mexican-American community:

a. *Spanish surname.* Although this seems to be the most common-sense criterion, the prevalence of Italian and French surnames often made this gauge inaccurate. A few examples of this can be mentioned. In the 1880 census, Rudi Conterno was listed as a Frenchman born in France of Italian parents. Silvas Mayo was born in Maine of native stock. Tomas Delano was born in Missouri of Italian parents. Difficulties such as these made it necessary to consider surname along with the place of birth.

b. *Place of birth.* If a person was born in Mexico or in California prior to 1848, he was classified as a Mexican-American. Although this measure seems clearcut, we should note that many persons were thus classified who did not have Spanish surnames. In 1880, for example, Anita Trudell, 50 years old, was a native-born Mexican whose father was English. Petra Johnson was also a native-born Mexican of Mexican parents. Guadalupe Broderick, 39 years old, was a native-born Californian whose parents had been born in Spain.

As clearcut as these criteria may seem, there were, in fact, many ambiguities in the censuses which made their strict application difficult. One example is Ignacio Fernandez, who was a native-born Guatemalan listed as a Negro in the census of 1870. I generally included those born in Latin America, Spain, and other regions of the Southwest if they met the Spanish-surname criterion. Children whose last names were not Spanish but who lived with Spanish-surnamed families presented another problem. The 1880 census, which listed family relationships, revealed that most of these chil-

dren were relatives—cousins, nephews, grandchildren,
etc. In a few cases they appeared to be illegitimate children. I followed the policy of classifying the non-
Spanish-surnamed children as Mexican-American if
their parents or family met the Mexican-American
criterion.

6. *Analysis of Mexican-American Family Relationships*

The censuses from 1850 to 1870 did not list family
relationships, but those taken in 1844 and 1880 did. The
problem I faced in trying to study the Mexican-
American family revolved around the difficulty of
filling in the information left out of the 1850, 1860, and
1870 censuses. Obvious relationships were apparent
from the listings by households. Most listings began
with the head of the household, followed by his wife
and children. There were, of course, many exceptions
to the nuclear family: parents, boarders, widows and
widowers, single men, siblings, illegitimate children,
common-law unions, guests, and visitors. These were
factors which had to be taken into account when
analyzing each household.

I began with the assumption that persons living
under the same roof constituted a family. I excluded
public dwellings such as hospitals, jails, hotels, and
rooming-houses, and followed a series of analytical
propositions in reconstructing the probable family
structure within each household:

a. Persons of the same last name were directly related.

b. The first person listed was the head of the household.

c. Subsequent persons of the same surname as the
householder were either a spouse, child, parent, or sibling, depending on their ages and sexes.

d. Those in the household with surnames differing
from the householder were either members of the extended family, boarders, or guests.

Other refinements were made to account for common-law unions and single men or women living together. Then each of these conditions was stated in a

computer program language (PL/1) and the census information was processed to determine family relationships. How accurate was this program in reconstructing family relationships? It should be emphasized that the reconstructed relationships were only probable and, like the census, contained a percentage of error associated with their generation. Comparing the computer-generated relationships with the actual relationships stated in the 1844 and 1880 censuses, I found that approximately 3 to 5 percent of the computer-generated relationships were in error. This is an acceptable range for the purpose of statistical analysis.

After the family relationships had been determined, I wrote another program to summarize the data for households and to divide the families into three types: nuclear, extended, and single families. Once summarized, the data was transferred to magnetic tape and then processed by a series of prepackaged programs.

While this research was underway, Professor Barbara Laslett published two studies analyzing the Los Angeles censuses of 1850 and 1870: "Household Structures on the American Frontier: Los Angeles, California, in 1850," *American Journal of Sociology,* July 1975; and "Social Change and the Family: Los Angeles, California, 1850–1870," *American Sociological Review,* April 1977. With the help of research assistants, Professor Laslett coded family relationships and employed a reliability code to determine the degree of probable error in her coding. She hypothesized five family types based on those used by Peter Laslett and Richard Wall in *Household and Family in Past Time,* p. 31. Her findings regarding the percentage of nuclear, extended, and single families differ slightly from mine for two reasons: (1) I defined families in terms of those living together under one roof in a household as determined by the census-taker, while she separated family units within the same household; consequently, Laslett found more than twice as many families in Los Angeles in 1850. (2) I used three family types while she used five, and this affected the difference in extended family percentages. Comparing the differences in our tabulations

of family types among the Spanish-speaking in Los
Angeles in 1850 shows that my computer-generated
family types differed from her hand-coded ones by
about 11 percent.

My term (Laslett's term)	Computer-Generated		Laslett Hand Coding	
	N	%	N	%
Single family (No family)	18	7.8%	34	9.1%
Nuclear family (Simple family)	52	22.4	140	37.3
Extended family (Simple family plus others) Extended family (Multiple family)	162	69.8	201	53.6

A point of contention will be whether or not my
extended-family definition is comparable to her definition of "simple family plus others" and "multiple family." I would assume a strong probability that the
"others" in the first type, and the members of the
"multiple family" in the second, were related to each
other, since they lived under the same roof. This point
is borne out by examination of the 1880 census, where
the household structure was found to be codetermi-
nate with the family. Laslett admits that her method
was unable to determine family extension through the
wife, and hence probably underenumerated extended
families.

Using different methodologies, we both reached es-
sentially the same conclusions regarding socioeconomic
trends among the Spanish-speaking. In sampling the
Los Angeles population in 1870 and comparing it to the
population in 1850, Laslett found the following: a general increase in laboring occupations, an increase in the
number of landless heads of families, an association of
propertied wealth with extended family backgrounds,
and an increase in the percentage of nuclear families.
All of these conclusions are supported by my analysis
of the data for Los Angeles Mexican-Americans.

APPENDIX B

Mexican-American Occupations, 1850–1880

The following computations were derived from an analysis of census returns for 1844–1880. Not included in this occupational breakdown are Anglo-American heads of households who intermarried with Mexican-Americans. Admittedly the census information regarding occupations was often ambiguous and incomplete. Undoubtedly some employed Mexican-Americans are missing from this sample.

There were many problems in classifying Mexican-American occupations. It was impossible from the census information alone to determine whether the individual was an employee or employer. It is very probable that some of those classified as skilled laborers also operated their own shops and belonged to the mercantile category as well. Those who were classified in mercantile occupations were those who seemed most clearly to be owners of commercial establishments. Occupations such as musician and policeman did not seem to fit into either the skilled, unskilled, or mercantile category and seemed closer to the professional group than to any other.

It is hard for a researcher not to project his own contemporary evaluation of occupational status into the past. But I have tried to list occupations according to how the Mexican-American community probably regarded them. A jailer, for example, because he had legal responsibilities and some authority over Anglos, probably was regarded as having the same status as a sheriff or even a lawyer. His position of prestige was even greater since he was the only keeper in town. For this reason he was classified as a professional.

Because of the many ambiguities and difficulties involved in classifying occupations, generalizations regarding occupational structure have only a hypothetical value. Slight changes in occupational distribution should not be magnified lest we compound the probable error of classification.

For a discussion of the technical problems involved in the construction of occupational categories, see the following: Peter K. Knights, *The Plain People of Boston, 1830–1860: A Study in City Growth,* ch. 5 and Appendix E; Stuart Blumin, "Mobility and Change in Ante-Bellum Philadelphia," in Thernstrom and Sennett (eds.), *Nineteenth-Century Cities: Essays in the New Urban History,* pp. 165–206; Edward Pessen, "The Occupations of the Ante-Bellum Rich: A Misleading Clue to the Source and Extent of Their Wealth," *Hist. Methods Newsletter;* Stephen Thernstrom, *Poverty and Progress,* pp. 91–93.

Tables 10 and 12 are based on the following categories:

A. Ranching and Agriculture

Agriculturalist	Vintner
Farmer	Livestock raiser
Gentleman	Orchardist
Grazier	

B. Professional

Clergyman	Assessor
Judge	Doctor
Teacher	Lawyer
Constable	Priest
Nun	Auditor
Editor	Justice of the Peace
Mayor	Oculist
Musician	Notary
Policeman	Nurse
Sheriff	

C. Mercantile

Clerk

Grocer

Merchant

Restaurateur

Trader

Druggist

Fruiter

Hotel-keeper

Saloon-keeper

Furniture dealer

Manufacturer

Miller

Peddler

D. Skilled Laborers

Apprentice

Baker

Blacksmith

Cabinetmaker

Carpenter

Cooper

Hatmaker

Locksmith

Mason

Saddler

Shoemaker

Soapmaker

Tailor

Watchmaker

Brewer

Brickmaker

Candymaker

Hatter

Painter

Plasterer

Printer

Barber

Tanner

Cigarmaker

Tinsmith

Brakeman

Collector

Conductor

Driller

Lamplighter

Mortar man

Saltmaker

Telegrapher

E. Unskilled Laborers

Laborer

Servant

Miner

Cook

Herdsman

Hunter

Laundress

Sailor

Teamster

Washerwoman

Stableman

Hackman

Paper boy

Plower

Well-digger

Woodcutter

APPENDIX C

The Los Angeles City Directories and Social Research

Many social historians have relied extensively on information contained in the nineteenth- and twentieth-century city directories. It is clear that these sources have many advantages over the census materials. The city directories are usually published annually and are readily accessible. They are in printed form, easy to read, and contain information on heads of households and residences not found in the censuses.

Despite their advantages, there is considerable debate over the accuracy of city directories in comparison with the United States censuses. Peter Knights, who has used the directories extensively, claims that some of them underenumerated from 20 to 30 percent of the population. He also found that they were less accurate than the censuses in counting the foreign-born and the poor.[1]

The city directories used in this study, particularly in Chapter 5, suffered from these deficiencies. In addition I found that the information they contained was occasionally inaccurate in that they often did not list the occupations of the heads of households. While I did not

1. Peter R. Knights, "City Directories as Aids to Ante-Bellum Urban Studies: A Research Note," *Hist. Methods Newsletter.*

use the directories to study social changes within the Mexican-American population, I did use these documents to plot residence patterns, since they were the only sources available.

A few observations on the quality of information contained in the directories compared to that found in the censuses is appropriate here. All indications are that the 1872 city directory grossly underenumerated the Mexican-American population. In that year, the directory counted 249 Spanish-surnamed heads of households. This was about half the number listed only two years earlier in the 1870 federal census (520 heads of households). It must be regarded as highly improbable that the Mexican-American population was cut in half in only two years.

The 1872 directory was also inaccurate in reporting occupational information. It listed the occupations of only 43 of the 207 male heads of households. The 1870 census listed the occupations of 315 (out of 451) male household heads. Again one would have to assume a fantastic and improbable decline in employment in order to use this directory for purposes of social analysis.

Unfortunately, no census data are available to check the accuracy of the 1887–88 city directory, but it appears to have been somewhat more accurate than the 1872 directory. It listed 392 Spanish-surnamed heads of households. Seven years earlier, the federal census listed 518 household heads. The 1887–88 directory was much more accurate than its predecessors in listing occupations. It counted 76 percent of the total number of heads of households as being employed. The 1880 census listed the occupations of only 67 percent of the household heads. Thus the city directories after 1880 may have been as accurate as the census in counting employment. It should be noted, however, that the directory of 1887–88 undercounted female heads of households (explaining why relatively more occupations were listed than earlier). In 1887–88 the directory company listed only about 13 percent of the household heads as being female. This was proportionately about a third of the percentage of female heads of household listed in the 1880 census. Possibly there was a decline in the proportion of women who headed families after 1880. A better explanation is that the directory neglected to count them.

From all this it appears that there is no one generalization that can be made regarding the various city directories of Los Angeles. Some were more accurate than others, depending on the year. Whatever their shortcomings, in relation to the censuses, they are still useful in providing large population samples to trace residential movements.

The directories can also be used to check directional hypotheses—ones that have been generated using census data. One such example of this use of the directories is a check I made of residential persistence. Using census information (see Chapter 2), I concluded that the Spanish-speaking had a declining rate of residential persistence—fewer and fewer tended to remain within the city limits as time progressed. I found that only about 9 percent of those families living in the city in 1860 continued to live there until 1880.

To check this hypothesis on geographic mobility, I sorted the city directory data for 1872 and 1887–88 by last name and, from this, determined what percentage of the Spanish-surnamed population listed in 1872 persisted until 1887–88. I found that only 27 of the 250 persons (11 percent) named in the 1872 directory continued to live in the pueblo. This seems to confirm my earlier hypothesis that the Mexican-American population was remarkably transient. It also indicates that their intensive mobility remained a feature of community life well into the 1880's and may have been a more or less permanent characteristic of their society.

GLOSSARY

abajeños: Mexicans living in Southern California prior to 1848

alcalde: a mayor of a town; sometimes acted as judge or civil magistrate

barrio: a region of a city or town where Mexicans, Chicanos, or other Spanish-speaking people live

Chicano: An American citizen born of Mexican-descent parents or a Mexican immigrant permanently residing in the United States

cholo: used in California to describe the low-caste Mexican soldiers prior to 1848; used after 1848 to describe working-class Mexicans or Mexican Americans

curandero: a healer who uses herbs and religious rituals

hacendados: owners of haciendas, large ranches or farms

hijos de pais: native sons, born in California before 1848

jacal: a small shelter built of sticks often adjoining an adobe

latifundian peonage: a labor system that forced landless workers to stay on large plantations or ranchos through hereditary debts owed to the hacendado

Mestizo: an ethnic group arising out of the intermarriage of the Spanish with the native Indian

norteños: Mexicans living in Northern California prior to 1848

pobladores: the first settlers, colonists of a town

pueblo: a small town or village

ranchería: a small settlement of Indians

rancheros: owners of ranches or haciendas

vaquero: a cowboy or herdsman

visitador: an official sent by the king of Spain to investigate the colonial administration in the New World

BIBLIOGRAPHY

Books

Acuña, Rudolfo. *Occupied America: The Chicano's Struggle Toward Liberation*. San Francisco: Canfield Press, 1972.

Allport, Gordon. *The Nature of Prejudice*. Cambridge, Mass.: Addison-Wesley, 1954.

Archdiocese of Los Angeles. *The Centennial, 1840–1940*. Los Angeles: Diocese of Los Angeles, 1940.

Ariès, Phillippe. *Centuries of Childhood*, trans. Robert Baldick. London: Jonathan Cape, 1962.

Armstrong, Barbara A. *California Family Law*. 2 vols. San Francisco: Bancroft Whitney, 1953.

Baker, B. Lea; Richard A. Wald; and Rita Zamora. *Economic Aspects of Mexican and Mexican-American Urban Households*. San Jose, Calif.: Institute of Business and Economic Research, 1971.

Bancroft, Hubert Howe. *California Pastoral, 1789–1848*. San Francisco: The History Book Company, 1888.

———. *The History of Arizona and New Mexico, 1530–1888*. San Francisco: The History Book Co., 1889.

———. *The History of California*. 7 vols. San Francisco: The History Book Co., 1884–90.

Barzun, Jacques, and Henry F. Graff. *The Modern Researcher: A Classic Manual on All Aspects of Research and Writing*, 2nd ed. New York: Harcourt, Brace and World, 1970.

Bell, Horace. *Reminiscences of a Ranger, or Early Times in Southern California* (1881). Santa Barbara, Calif.: Wallace Hebberd, 1927.

Bendix, Reinhard, and Seymour Martin Lipset, eds. *Class, Status and Power: Social Stratification in Comparative Perspective*. Glencoe, Ill.: Free Press, 1953.

Blanco, Antonio S. *La Lengua Española en la Historia de California: Contribución a Su Estudio*. Madrid: Ediciones Cúltura Hispanica, 1971.

Blau, Peter M., and Otis Duncan. *The American Occupational Structure.* New York: Wiley, 1964.

Blauner, Robert. *Racial Oppression in America.* New York: Harper and Row, 1972.

Calderon de la Barca, Frances E. *Life in Mexico During a Residence of Two Years in That Country.* London: Chapman and Hall, 1843.

Caromonías, J. *Diccionario Crítico: Etimológico de la Lengua Castellana.* Berne, Switzerland: Editorial Francke, 1954.

Castillo, Pedro, and Albert Camarillo, eds. *Furia y Muerte: Los Bandidos Chicanos.* Monograph no. 4. Chicano Studies Center, Aztlán Publications, University of California Los Angeles, 1973.

Caughey, John W. *California,* 2nd ed. Englewood Cliffs, N.J.: Prentice-Hall, 1953.

————, ed. *The Indians of Southern California in 1852: The B. D. Wilson Report and a Selection of Contemporary Comment.* San Marino, Calif.: The Huntington Library, 1952.

Clark, Margaret. *Health in the Mexican-American Culture: A Community Study.* Berkeley and Los Angeles: University of California Press, 1969.

Cleland, Robert Glass. *The Cattle on a Thousand Hills: Southern California, 1850–1880.* San Marino, Calif.: The Huntington Library, 1941.

Coale, A. J., and E. M. Hoover. *Population Growth and Economic Development in Low-Income Countries.* Princeton, N.J.: Princeton University Press, 1958.

Cole, M. R. *Los Pastores: A Mexican Play of the Nativity.* New York: Houghton Mifflin, 1909.

Collins, Randall. *Conflict Sociology: Towards an Explanatory Science.* New York: Academic Press, 1975.

Coser, Lewis A. *The Functions of Social Conflict,* 2nd ed. New York: Free Press, 1964.

Cumming, Elaine, and David Schneider. *A Social Profile of Detroit.* Ann Arbor: Department of Sociology and Survey Research Center, University of Michigan, 1957.

Dakin, Susanna Bryant. *The Lives of William Hartnell.* Stanford, Calif.: Stanford University Press, 1949.

————. *A Scotch Paisano: Hugo Reid's Life in California, 1832–1852: Derived from his Correspondence.* Los Angeles and Berkeley: University of California Press, 1939.

Demos, John. *A Little Commonwealth: Family Life in Plymouth Colony.* New York: Oxford University Press, 1970.

De Toro, Juan. *A Brief Sketch of the Colonization of California and Foundation of the Pueblo of Our Lady of Los Angeles.* Los Angeles: Daily Commercial Job Printing House, 1882.

Dobie, Frank. *Guide to Life and Literature of the Southwest.* Austin: University of Texas Press, 1943.

Duran, Livie Isaura, and H. Russell Bernard, eds. *Introduction to Chicano Studies: A Reader.* New York: Macmillan, 1973.

Ellison, William H., and Francis Price, eds. *The Life and Adventures of Don Augustin Janssens, 1834–1856.* San Marino, Calif.: The Huntington Library, 1953.

Firth, Aamon. *Two Studies of Kinship in London.* London: Athlene Press, 1956.

Fogelson, Robert. *The Fragmented Metropolis: Los Angeles, 1850–1930.* Cambridge, Mass.: Harvard University Press, 1967.

Forbes, Jack D. *Aztecas del Norte: The Chicanos of Aztlán.* Greenwich, Conn.: Fawcett Publications, 1973.

Fromm, Erich, and Michael Macoby. *Social Character in a Mexican Village: A Sociopsychoanalytical Study.* Englewood Cliffs, N.J.: Prentice-Hall, 1970.

Gamio, Manuel. *Mexican Immigration to the United States.* Chicago: University of Chicago Press, 1930.

Geary, Gerald. *The Transfer of Ecclesiastical Jurisdiction in California, 1840–1853.* Washington, D.C.; Catholic University of America, 1932.

George, Henry. *Our Land and Our Land Policy, National and State.* San Francisco: White and Bauer Publishers, 1871.

Gibson, Charles. *Los Aztecas bajo el domino Español, 1519–1810,* trans. Julieta Campos. Mexico: Siglo Veintiuno Editores, 1967.

Glass, David V., and David E. C. Eversley, eds. *Population in History.* Chicago: Aldine Publ. Co., 1965.

Gordon, Milton M. *Assimilation in American Life: The Role of Race, Religion and National Origins.* New York: Oxford University Press, 1964.

Grebler, Leo. *The Mexican Immigration to the United States: The Record and Its Implications.* Mexican–American Study Project, Advance Report no. 2. Los Angeles: Graduate School of Business Administration, University of California, 1966.

Greenwood, Robert, and George A. Beers. *The California*

Outlaw: Tiburcio Vasquez. Los Gatos, Calif.: Talisman Press, 1960.

Greven, Phillip J. *Four Generations: Population, Land and Family in Colonial Andover, Massachusetts.* Ithaca, N.Y.: Cornell University Press, 1970.

Guinn, James M. *A History of California and an Extended History of Los Angeles and Environs.* 2 vols. Los Angeles: Historic Records Co., 1915.

Handlin, Oscar. *Immigration as a Factor in American History.* Englewood Cliffs, N.J.: Prentice-Hall, 1959.

Hansen, Woodrow J. *The Search for Authority in California.* Oakland, Calif.: Biobooks, 1960.

Hareven, Tamara K., ed. *Anonymous Americans: Explorations in Nineteenth Century Social History.* Englewood Cliffs, N.J.: Prentice-Hall, 1971.

Hastings, Lansford Warren. *The Emigrants Guide to Oregon and California, Reproduced in Facsimile from Original 1845 Edition.* Princeton: Princeton University Press, 1932.

Hauser, Phillip M., and Otis Dudley Duncan, eds. *The Study of Population: An Inventory and Appraisal.* Chicago: University of Chicago Press, 1959.

Hayes, Benjamin. *Pioneer Notes, 1849–1875.* Los Angeles: Marjorie Tisdale Wocott, 1929.

Heizer, Robert F., ed. *The Indians of Los Angeles County: Hugo Reid's Letters of 1852.* Southwest Museum Papers, No. 21. Highland Park, California: Southwest Museum, 1968.

———, and M. A. Whipple, eds. *The California Indians: A Source Book.* Berkeley and Los Angeles: University of California Press, 1951.

Hill, Laurence L. *La Reina: Los Angeles in Three Centuries.* Los Angeles: Security Trust and Savings Bank, 1889.

Hobsbawm, Eric J. *Primitive Rebels: Studies in Archaic Forms of Social Movement in the Nineteenth and Twentieth Centuries.* New York: Praeger, 1959.

Hutchinson, C. Alan. *Frontier Settlement in Mexican California: The Padres–Hijar Colony.* New Haven, Conn.: Yale University Press, 1969.

Hutchinson, Edward P. *Immigrants and Their Children.* New York: Wiley, 1956.

Johnston, Bernice E. *California's Gabrielino Indians.* Los Angeles: Southwest Museum, 1962.

Knights, Peter R. *The Plain People of Boston, 1830–1860: A Study in City Growth.* New York: Oxford University Press, 1971.

Kroeber, Alfred L. *Handbook of the Indians of California.* Washington: Government Printing Office, 1925.

Laslett, Peter, and Richard Wall, eds. *Household and Family in Past Time.* Cambridge, Eng.: Cambridge University Press, 1972.

Leonard, Olen, and E. P. Loomis. *The Culture of a Contemporary Rural Community: El Cerrito, New Mexico.* Rural Life Studies no. 1. Washington, D.C.: U.S. Department of Agriculture, 1941.

Lewis, Oscar. *Life in a Mexican Village: Tepoztlan Restudied,* 2nd ed. Urbana: University of Illinois Press, 1963.

Lockridge, Kenneth. *Literacy in Colonial New England: An Inquiry into the Social Context of Literacy in the Early Modern West.* New York: Norton, 1974.

Loosley, Allyn C. *The Foreign-Born Population of California, 1848–1920.* Report, 1927. San Francisco: R and E Research Associates, 1971.

Lopez y Rivas, Gilberto. *The Chicanos: Life and Struggles of the Mexican Minority in the United States.* New York: Monthly Review Press, 1973.

Madsen, William. *The Mexican-Americans of South Texas.* New York: Holt, Rinehart and Winston, 1964.

Malthus, Thomas. *First Essay on Population, 1798.* New York: E. P. Dutton Co., 1914.

McGloin, John Bernard. *California's First Archbishop: The Life of Joseph Sadoc Alemany, O.P.* New York: Herder and Herder, 1966.

McWilliams, Carey. *North from Mexico: The Spanish-Speaking People of the United States,* 2nd ed. Westport, Conn.: Greenwood Press, 1968.

Meier, Matt S., and Feliciano Rivera. *The Chicanos, A History of Mexican-Americans.* New York: Hill and Wang, 1972.

Meyer, Michael C. *Huerta: A Political Portrait.* Lincoln: University of Nebraska Press, 1971.

Moore, Joan W., and Frank G. Mittlebach. *Residential Segregation in the Urban Southwest.* Mexican-American Study Project, Advance Report no. 4. Los Angeles: Graduate School of Business Administration, University of California, 1967.

Moquin, Wayne, and Charles Van Doren, eds. *A Documentary History of the Mexican-Americans.* New York: Praeger, 1971.

Mora, Jo. *Californios.* New York: Doubleday, 1949.

Morgan, Edmund. *The Puritan Family: Religion and Domestic Relations in Seventeenth-Century New England.* Boston: Boston Public Library, 1947 (reprint, 1966).

Murray, Sister Mary John. *A Socio-Cultural Study of 118 Mexican Families Living in a Low-Rent Housing Project in San Antonio, Texas.* Washington, D.C.: Catholic University of America Press, 1954.

Nadeau, Remi A. *City Makers: The Men Who Transformed Los Angeles from a Village to a Metropolis During the First Great Boom, 1868–1876.* New York: Doubleday, 1948.

Navarro, Moises Gonzales. *La Colonización en Mexico, 1877–1910.* Mexico, 1960.

Newmark, Marco. *Jottings in Southern California History.* Los Angeles: Ward Ritchie Press, 1955.

Newmark, Maurice H., and Marco R. Newmark. *The Census of Los Angeles, 1850.* Los Angeles: Times–Mirror Press, 1929.

———, eds. *Sixty Years in Southern California, 1853–1913: Containing the Reminiscences of Harris Newmark.* Los Angeles: Zeitlin and Ver Brugge, 1970.

Nie, Norman H.; Dale H. Bent; and Cahdlai Hyll. *SPSS: Statistical Package for the Social Sciences.* New York: McGraw Hill, 1970

Ord, Angustias de la Guerra. *Occurrences in Hispanic California,* trans. Francis Price and William Ellison. Washington, D.C.: Academy of Franciscan History, 1956.

Osofsky, Gilbert. *Harlem, The Making of a Ghetto: Negro New York 1890–1930.* New York: Harper and Row, 1963.

Packman, Ana Begue. *Leather Dollars: Short Stories of the Pueblo of Los Angeles.* Los Angeles: Times–Mirror Press, 1932.

Palm, Charles W., and Edward N. Buck, eds. *Political Statistician.* Los Angeles: The Daily Journal, 1892.

Park, Robert E. *The Immigrant Press and Its Social Control.* Westport, Conn.: Greenwood Press, 1970.

———. *Human Communities.* New York: Stratford Press, 1952.

————, and Herbert A. Miller. *Old World Traits Transplanted.* New York: Harper, 1921.

————. *On Social Control and Collective Behavior.* Chicago: University of Chicago Press, 1967.

La Patria de Los Angeles. *Ricardo della Colonia Italiana del Sud della California.* Los Angeles: La Patria de Los Angeles, 1915.

Pessen, Edward, ed. *Three Centuries of Social Mobility in America.* Lexington, Mass.: Heath, 1974.

Pitt, Leonard. *The Decline of the Californios: A Social History of the Spanish-Speaking Californians, 1846–1890.* Berkeley and Los Angeles: University of California Press, 1970.

Prago, Albert. *Strangers in Their Own Land: A History of Mexican-Americans.* New York: Four Winds Press, 1973.

Redfield, Robert. *Tepoztlan: A Mexican Village.* Chicago: University of Chicago Press, 1930.

Reid, Hugo. *The Indians of Los Angeles County.* Los Angeles: Glen Dawson Press, 1952.

Robinson, Alfred. *Life in California: A Historical Account of the Origin, Customs and Traditions of the Indians of Alta California* (1846). Oakland, Calif.: Biobooks, 1947.

Robinson, William Wilcox. *The Indians of Los Angeles: The Story of the Liquidation of a People.* Los Angeles: Glen Dawson Press, 1952.

————. *Land in California.* Los Angeles and Berkeley: University of California Press, 1948.

————. *The Lawyers of Los Angeles.* Los Angeles: Los Angeles Bar Association, 1959.

————. *Los Angeles from the Days of the Pueblo.* San Francisco: California Historical Society, 1959.

————. *Maps of Los Angeles: From Ord's Survey of 1849 to the End of the Boom of the 80's.* Los Angeles: Dawson's Book Shop, 1962.

————. *The People vs. Lugo.* Los Angeles: Dawson's Book Shop, 1962.

————. *Ranchos Become Cities.* Pasadena, Calif.: San Pasqual Press, 1939.

————. *Tarnished Angels: Paradisical Turpitude in Los Angeles Revealed.* Los Angeles: Ward Ritchie Press, 1964.

Rostow, Walter W. *The Stages of Economic Growth: A Non-Communist Manifesto.* New York and London: Cambridge University Press, 1961.

Rowney, Don Karl, and James Q. Graham, Jr., eds. *Quantita-*

tive History: Selected Reading in the Quantitative Analysis of Historical Data. Homewood, Ill.: Dorsey Press, 1969.

Royce, Josiah. *California from Conquest in 1848 to the Second Vigilance Committee in San Francisco: A Study in American Character,* 2nd ed. New York: Knopf, 1948.

Samora, Julian, ed. *La Raza, Forgotten Americans.* Notre Dame, Ind.: University of Notre Dame Press, 1966.

Samora, Julian, and Richard A. Lamanna. *Mexican Americans in a Midwest Metropolis: A Study of East Chicago.* Mexican-American Study Project, Advance Report no. 8. Los Angeles: Graduate School of Business Administration, University of California, 1967.

Sawyer, Eugene T. *The Life and Career of Tiburcio Vasquez.* San Francisco: Bacon Co., 1875.

Scheiner, Seth. *Negro Mecca.* New York: New York University Press, 1965.

Sennett, Richard. *Families Against the City: Middle-Class Homes of Industrial Chicago, 1872–1890.* Cambridge, Mass.: Harvard University Press, 1970.

Servin, Manuel, ed. *An Awakened Minority: The Mexican Americans,* 2nd ed. Beverly Hills, Calif.: Glencoe Press, 1970.

Shevky, Eshref, and Wendell Bell. *Social Area Analysis: Theory, Illustrative Application and Computational Procedures.* Stanford, Calif.: Stanford University Press, 1955.

————, and Marylin Williams. *The Social Areas of Los Angeles: Analysis and Typology.* Berkeley and Los Angeles: University of California Press, 1949.

Shibutani, Tamotsu, and Kian W. Kwan. *Ethnic Stratification: A Comparative Approach.* New York: Macmillan, 1972.

Smith, Adam. *An Inquiry into the Nature and Causes of the Wealth of Nations,* ed. George J. Stigler. New York: Appleton-Century-Crofts, 1957.

Smith, Lynn T. *The Fundamentals of Population Study.* Philadelphia: Lippincott, 1966.

Social Science Research Council, eds. *The Statistical History of the United States from Colonial Times to the Present,* 3rd ed. Stamford, Conn.: Fairfield, 1965.

Sorokin, Pitirim. *Social Mobility.* New York: Harper, 1927.

Spear, Allan. *Black Chicago: The Making of a Negro Ghetto.* Chicago: University of Chicago Press, 1965.

Stonequist, Everett V. *The Marginal Man: A Study in Person-*

ality and Culture Conflict. New York: Russell and Russell, 1961.

Stoughton, Gertrude. *The Books of California.* Los Angeles: Ward Ritchie Press, 1968.

Swadish, Frances Leon. *Los Primeros Pobladores: Hispanic Americans of the Ute Frontier.* Notre Dame, Ind.: University of Notre Dame Press, 1974.

Thernstrom, Stephen. *Poverty and Progress.* Cambridge, Mass.: Atheneum Press, 1964.

————. *The Other Bostonians: Poverty and Progress in the American Metropolis.* Cambridge, Mass.: Harvard University Press, 1973.

————, and Richard Sennett, eds. *Nineteenth-Century Cities: Essays in the New Urban History.* New Haven, Conn.: Yale University Press, 1969.

Thompson, Thomas H.; Augustus West; and J. Albert Wilson. *History of Los Angeles County, California, with Illustrations* (1880), 2nd ed. Berkeley, Calif.: Howell-North, 1959.

Thompson, Warren S. *Growth and Change in California's Population.* Los Angeles: The Haynes Foundation, 1955.

Thornthwaite, Warren C. *Internal Migration in the United States.* Philadelphia: University of Pennsylvania Press, 1934.

Vorspan, Max, and Lloyd P. Gartner. *A History of the Jews in Los Angeles.* San Marino, Calif.: The Huntington Library, 1970.

Wagner, Nathaniel N., and Marsha J. Huang, eds. *Chicanos: Social and Psychological Perspectives.* St. Louis, Mo.: C. V. Mosby Co., 1971.

Warner, Col. Juan J. *An Historical Sketch of Los Angeles County,* 2nd ed. Los Angeles: O. W. Smith, 1936.

Warner, W. Lloyd; Marsha Meeker; and Kenneth Eelks. *Social Class in America: A Manual of Procedure for the Study of the Measurement of Social Status.* Chicago: Social Science Research Associates, 1949.

Weber, David J., ed. *Foreigners in Their Native Land: Historical Roots of the Mexican-Americans.* Albuquerque: University of New Mexico Press, 1973.

Weber, Rev. Francis J. *A Biographical Sketch of Rt. Rev. Francisco García y Moreno, the First Bishop of the Californias, 1775–1846.* Los Angeles: The Barromeno Guild, 1961.

————. *California's Reluctant Prelate: The Life and Times of Rt. Rev. Thaddeus Amat, C.M. 1811–1878*. Los Angeles: Dawson's Book Shop, 1964.

————. *Catholic Footprints in California*. Newhall, Calif.: Hogarth Press, 1970.

————. *Francisco Mora, Last of the Catalans*. Los Angeles: Westerlore Press, 1967.

————. *El Pueblo de los Angeles: An Enquiry in Early Appellations*. Los Angeles: Archdiocese of Los Angeles, 1968.

————. *Rt. Rev. Joseph Sadoc Alemany, O.P., Bishop of Monterey*. Van Nuys, California: California Historical Publications, 1961.

————. *A Select Los Angeles Bibliography*. Los Angeles: Dawson's Book Shop, 1970.

Willard, Charles D. *Herald's History of Los Angeles City*. Los Angeles: Kinsley-Barnes and Newman Co., 1901.

Wrigley, Edward A. *Population and History*. New York: McGraw-Hill, 1969.

Journal Articles

Alvarez, Salvador. "Mexican-American Community Organizations." *El Grito* 4, no. 3 (Spring 1971): 68–77.

Bell, Wendell. "A Probability Model for the Measurement of Ecological Segregation." *Social Forces* 32, no. 4 (May 1954): 357–364.

Berent, Jerzy. "Fertility and Social Mobility." *Population Studies* 5, no. 3 (March 1952): 244–260.

Blau, Peter M. "Social Mobility and Interpersonal Relations." *American Sociological Review* 21 (1956): 290–295.

Blauner, Robert. "Internal Colonization and Ghetto Revolt." *Social Problems* 16, no. 4 (Spring 1969): 393–408.

Blumin, Stewart. "The Historical Study of Vertical Mobility." *Historical Methods Newsletter* 1, no. 4 (September 1968): 1–13.

Breshard, Marcel. "Mobilité Sociale et Dimension de la Famille." *Population* 3 (July–September 1950): 533–535.

Campbell, Leon G. "The First Californios: Presidial Society in Spanish California, 1769–1822." *Journal of the West* 11, no. 4 (October 1972): 582–595.

Charles, William N. "The Transcription of and Translation of Old Mexican Documents of the Los Angeles County Archives." *Quarterly of the Historical Society of Southern California* 20, no. 2 (June 1938): 84–88.

Cumming, Elaine, and David Schneider. "Sibling Solidarity: A Property of American Kinship." *American Anthropologist* 63 (1961): 489–507.

Dawson, Muir. "Southern California Newspapers, 1851–1876, Part I." *Quarterly of the Historical Society of Southern California* 32 (March 1950): 5–44.

Dumond, David E. "Population Growth and Cultural Change." *Southwest Journal of Anthropology* 21, no. 4 (Winter 1968): 302–324.

Duncan, Otis Dudley, and Beverly Duncan. "Methodological Analysis of Segregation Indexes." *American Sociological Review* 20, no. 2 (April 1955): 213–217.

———. "Residential Distribution and Occupational Stratification." *Journal of Sociology* 60 (March 1955): 493–503.

García, Mario. "The Californios of San Diego and the Politics of Accommodation." *Aztlán: International Journal of Chicano Studies Research* 6, no. 1 (Spring 1975): 69–85.

Garr, Daniel J. "A Rare and Desolate Land: Population and Race in Hispanic California." *Western Historical Quarterly* 6, no. 2 (April 1975): 134–148.

Glasco, Lawrence. "Computerizing the Manuscript Census," in 2 parts. *Historical Methods Newsletter* 3, no. 1 (December 1969): 1–4; no. 2 (March 1970): 20–25.

Glazer, Walter S. Review of *Families Against the Cities: Middle Class Homes of Industrial Chicago, 1872–1890* by Richard Sennett. *Journal of American History* 68, no. 1 (February 1972): 213.

Graff, Harvey J. "Notes on Methods for Studying Literacy from the Manuscript Census." *Historical Methods Newsletter* 5, no. 1 (December 1971): 11–16.

Griswold del Castillo, Richard. "Health and the Mexican-Americans in Los Angeles, 1850–1887." *Journal of Mexican-American History* 4 (1974): 19–27.

de la Guerra, Pablo. "Address Before the California State Legislature." *El Grito* 5, no. 1 (Fall 1971): 19–22.

Guinn, James M. "The Siege and Capture of Los Angeles, 1846." *Annual of the Historical Society of Southern California* 3 (1893): 47–62.

———. "The Old Pueblo Archives." *Quarterly of the Historical Society of Southern California* 4 (1896): 37–42.

———. "Old-Time Schools and School Masters of Los Angeles." *Annual of the Historical Society of Southern California* 3 (1896): 7–16.

————. "Pioneer School Superintendents." *Quarterly of the Historical Society of Southern California* 4 (1896): 76–84.

Hughes, Charles. "The Decline of the Californios: The Case of San Diego, 1846–1856." *Journal of San Diego History* 21, no. 2 (Spring 1975): 1–31.

Humphrey, Norman D. "The Changing Structure of the Detroit Mexican Family." *American Sociological Review* 9, no. 6 (1944): 622–626.

Janowitz, Morris. "Some Consequences of Social Mobility in the United States." *Transactions of the Third World Congress of Sociology* 3 (1956): 291–301.

Johnson, Sigurd. "Family Organization in Spanish-American Culture Areas." *Sociology and Social Research* 28 (September–October 1943): 123–131.

————. "Social Organization of Spanish-American Villages." *Southwestern Social Science Quarterly* 23, no. 1 (June 1942): 151–159.

Knights, Peter R. "A Method for Estimating Census Under-Enumeration." *Historical Methods Newsletter* 4, no. 1 (March 1970): 5–8.

————. "City Directories as Aids to Ante-Bellum Urban Studies: A Research Note." *Historical Methods Newsletter* 2, no. 3 (September 1969): 1–9.

Laslett, Barbara. "Household Structures on the American Frontier: Los Angeles, California, in 1850." *American Journal of Sociology* 81, no. 1 (July 1975): 107–128.

————. "Social Change and the Family: Los Angeles, California, 1850–1870." *American Sociological Review* 42, no. 2 (April 1977): 268–290.

Laurie, Bruce; Theodore Hershberg; and George Alter. "Immigrants and Industry: The Philadelphia Experience, 1850–1880." *Journal of Social History* 9, no. 2 (Winter 1970): 240–243.

Layne, J. Gregg, comp. "The First Census of the Los Angeles District." *Quarterly of the Historical Society of Southern California* (September–December 1936): 81–114.

Lugo, José Carmen del. "Vida de un ranchero . . . ," trans. Helen Pruitt Beattie. *Quarterly of the Historical Society of Southern California* 31, no. 3 (September 1950): 185–236.

Marcella, Gabriel. "Spanish-Mexican Contributions to the Southwest." *Journal of Mexican-American History* 1 (Fall 1970): 1–11.

Martinez, Oscar. "On the Size of the Chicano Population: New Estimates, 1850–1890." *Aztlán: International Journal of Chicano Studies Research* 4, no. 1 (Spring 1975): 43–67.

May, Ernest. "Tiburcio Vasquez." *Quarterly of the Historical Society of Southern California* 29–30 (September–December 1947): 18–19.

Moore, Joan W. "Colonization and the Mexican-Americans." *Social Problems* 18, no. 4 (Spring 1970): 463–472.

Navarro, Joseph. "The Condition of Mexican-American History." *Journal of Mexican-American History* 1 (Fall 1970): 24–25.

Newcombe, H. B. "Record Linking: The Design for Linking Records into Individual and Family Histories." *American Journal of Human Genetics* 29 (1967): 339–359.

Northrup, Marie E., comp. "The Los Angeles Padrón of 1844." *Quarterly of the Historical Society of Southern California* 42, no. 4 (December 1960): 360–414.

Peñalosa, Fernando. "Mexican Family Roles." *Journal of Marriage and the Family* 38 (November 1968): 680–689.

———. "Towards an Operational Definition of the Mexican-American." *Aztlán: Chicano Journal of Social Sciences and the Arts* 1, no. 2 (Spring 1970): 1–11.

Pessen, Edward. "The Occupations of the Ante-Bellum Rich: A Misleading Clue to the Sources and Extent of Their Wealth." *Historical Methods Newsletter* 5, no. 2 (March 1972): 49–51.

Pitt, Leonard. "The Beginnings of Nativism in California." *Pacific Historical Review* 30 (February 1961): 23–38.

Ramírez, Francisco P. "A Mí María Antonia." *El Grito* 4, no. 1 (Fall 1971): 23.

Ríos, C. Herminio. "Towards a True Chicano Bibliography, Part II." *El Grito* 4, no. 4 (Summer 1972): 38–47.

Riss, Jean F. "The Lynching of Francisco Torres." *Journal of Mexican-American History*: 90–112.

Robinson, William W. "The Indians of Los Angeles as Revealed by the Los Angeles City Archives." *Quarterly of the Historical Society of Southern California* 20 (December 1938): 156–172.

Romano, Octavio I. "Donship in a Mexican-American Community in Texas." *American Anthropologist* 62 (1960): 966–976.

————. "Social Science, Objectivity and the Chicanos." *El Grito* 4, no. 1 (Fall 1970): 4–14.

Skolnich, M. S. "A Computer Program for Linking Records." *Historical Methods Newsletter* 4, no. 4 (September 1971): 114–125.

Smith, T. Lynn. "Current Population Trends in Latin America." *American Journal of Sociology* 62, no. 4 (1949): 399–406.

Staples, Robert. "The Mexican-American Family: Its Modification Over Time and Space." *Phylon* (Second Summer Quarter 1971): 179–192.

Temple, Thomas Workman II. "Soldiers and Settlers of the Expedition of 1781." *Quarterly of the Historical Society of Southern California* 15 (1931–1933): 99–104.

Ward, David. "The Emergence of Central Immigrant Ghettos in American Cities, 1840–1920." *Annals of the Association of American Geographers* 58 (June 1968): 343–359.

Waters, Otis Willard. "1861–1876 Los Angeles Bibliography," in 2 parts. *Quarterly of the Historical Society of Southern California,* 19, no. 2 (June 1937): 63–94; 20, no. 2 (June 1939): 60–83.

Weber, David J. "Mexico's Far Northern Frontier, 1821–1854: Historiography Askew." *Western Historical Quarterly* 7, no. 2 (July 1976): 292–293.

Westoff, Charles; Marvin Bressler; and Phillip C. Sagi. "The Concept of Social Mobility: An Empirical Inquiry." *American Sociological Review* 25 (June 1960): 375–380.

Winchester, Ian. "The Linkage of Historical Records by Man and Computer: Techniques and Problems." *Journal of Inter-Disciplinary History* (1970): 107–124.

Wright, Doris M. "The Making of Cosmopolitan California: An Analysis of Immigration, 1848–1870." *California Historical Quarterly* 19, no. 4 (December 1940): 323–325.

Dissertations and Theses

Broadbent, Elizabeth. "The Distribution of the Mexican Population in the United States." Master's thesis, Geography, University of Chicago, 1941.

Broshart, Kay Richards. "Social Class, Occupational Mobility, Migration and Nuclear Family Relations: A Study of the Nuclear Family's Use of Help." Ph.D. dissertation, Sociology, Yale University, 1968.

Gonzales, Kathleen. "The Mexican Family in San Antonio." Master's thesis, University of Texas, Austin, 1928.

Hogue, Edwin. "A History of Religion in Southern California." Ph.D. dissertation, History, Columbia University, 1968.

Lacy, Eloise. "Contributions of People of French Origin to the History of Los Angeles." Master's thesis, History, University of Southern California, 1946.

Lewis, Albert Lucian. "Los Angeles in the Civil War Decades, 1850–1868." Ph.D. dissertation, History, University of Southern California, 1970.

Meldrum, George Weston. "The History of the Treatment of Foreign and Minority Groups in California, 1830–1860." Ph.D. dissertation, History, Stanford University, 1948.

Mitchell, Richard. "Joaquin Murieta: A Study of Social Conditions in Early California." Master's thesis, History, University of California, Berkeley, 1927.

Morefield, Richard Henry. "Mexican Adaptation in American California 1846–1857." Master's thesis, History, University of California, Berkeley, 1955.

Nostrand, Richard Lee. "The Hispanic-American Borderlands: A Regional Historical Geography." Ph.D. dissertation, Geography, University of California, Los Angeles, 1968.

Peñalosa, Fernando. "Class Consciousness and Social Mobility in a Mexican-American Community." Ph.D. dissertation, Sociology, University of Southern California, 1963.

Phillips, Robert N. "Los Angeles Spanish: A Descriptive Analysis." Ph.D. dissertation, Linguistics, University of Michigan, 1967.

Pitt, Leonard. "The Submergence of the Mexican in California, 1846–1890: A History of Culture Conflict and Acculturation." Ph.D. dissertation, History, University of California, Los Angeles, 1958.

Prior, Edward Thomas, Jr. "Family Structure and Change: Rhode Island 1857–1960." Ph.D. dissertation, Sociology, Brown University, 1967.

Tays, George. "Revolutionary California: The Political History of California During the Mexican Period 1822–1846." Ph.D. dissertation, History, University of California, Berkeley, 1955.

Toto, Charles, Jr. "A History of Education in California, 1800–1850." Ph.D. dissertation, History, University of California, Berkeley, 1967.

Newspapers and Broadsides

El Aguacero, 1878.
El Amigo del Pueblo, 1861–1862.
El Clamor Público, 1855–1859.
La Crónica, 1872–1883.
El Demócrata, 1882.
Las Dos Repúblicas, 1892–1896.
El Eco Mexicano, 1885.
La Estrella, 1851–1855.
La Fé en la Democracia, 1884.
El Joven, 1877–1878.
Los Angeles News, 1856.
Los Angeles Star, 1851–1860.
El Monitor Mexicano, 1895.
The Pacific, 1851.
La Revista Hispano-Americana, 1892.
Special Program for Mexican Independence Day, September 15–16, 1887.
La Verdad, n.d.
La Voz de la Justicia, 1876.

Manuscripts and Documents

IN THE BANCROFT LIBRARY, UNIVERSITY OF CALIFORNIA, BERKELEY:

Amador, José María. *Memorias sobre la Historia de California.* 1877.
Arnaz, José. *Recuerdos.* 1877.
Botello, Narciso. *Anales del Sur de la California.* January 27, 1878.
Coronel, Antonio. *Cosas de California.* 1877.
Documentos para la Historia de California, Archivos de la Familia Requena.
Pico, Pío. *Narración historica.* 1877.
Pronunciamento de Varela y otros Californios contra los Americanos, 1846.

IN THE CALIFORNIA STATE LIBRARY, SACRAMENTO:

Daughters of the American Revolution. *The California State Census of 1852.* (Typescript and microfilm.)

IN THE FEDERAL RECORDS CENTER, LOS ANGELES:

Garcia, Regan R. "Archives Report, March 15, 1971." (Typescript.)
U.S. District Court, Southern Section. "Criminal Cases, 1887–1905," vol. 1.
———. "Jury Roll," vol. 1, 1887–1896.
———. "Register of Criminal Cases 1887–1905," vol. 1.
———. "Rolls of Attorneys from June 13, 1887, to November 9, 1925."

IN THE HUNTINGTON LIBRARY, SAN MARINO:

The Stearns Collection.

IN THE LOS ANGELES COUNTY MUSEUM OF NATURAL HISTORY:

Assessment Book for the Property of Los Angeles County, City, for the Years 1876,1885, and 1886.
Assessment Roll for the County of Los Angeles, City, 1861.
Coronel Collection.
Del Valle Collection.
"Lists of Grand and Trial Jurors, 1863–1873."
"School Board Reports, Bonds, etc."

IN LOS ANGELES COUNTY OFFICES:

Los Angeles County Clerk's Office, Superior Court, Criminal Division. "Criminal Complaints, 1887." (Microfilm.)
Los Angeles County Recorder's Office. *Index to Marriage Certificates, 1851–1876,* vol. 1.
———. *Index to Marriage Certificates, 1876–1886,* vol. 2.
———. *Index to Deaths, 1877–1887,* vol. 1.
Los Angeles Superior Court. "Articles of Incorporation of La Sociedad Hispano-Americana, December 9, 1875."

IN THE LOS ANGELES PUBLIC LIBRARY:

Dorsey, Susan M. "History of Schools and Education in Los Angeles." (Typescript.) n.d.

IN THE NATIONAL ARCHIVES, WASHINGTON, D.C.:

Population Schedules of the Eighth Census of the United States, 1860. (Microfilm.)
Population Schedules of the Ninth Census of the United States, 1870. (Microfilm.)
Population Schedules of the Tenth Census of the United States, 1880. (Microfilm.)

PRIVATELY PRINTED LETTER:

Letter from John S. Griffen, M.D., to Col. J. D. Stevenson, March 11, 1849. Los Angeles: privately printed, 1949.

PUBLISHED DIRECTORIES:

The First Los Angeles City and County Directory, 1872, ed. Ward Ritchie with an Introduction by James M. Guinn. Los Angeles: Ward Ritchie Press, 1963.
Los Angeles City Directory, 1887–1888. Los Angeles: Los Angeles Directory Co., 1888.

IN UNIVERSITY OF CALIFORNIA, LOS ANGELES, SPECIAL COLLECTIONS:

Genealogical Records Committee of California, State Society of the Daughters of the American Revolution Mss. *Libro de bautismos de N.S. de Los Angeles en la ciudad de Los Angeles,* libros I–IV. (Typescript.) 1945.

Government Publications

California Legislature. *Journal of the 4th Session: January 1853–May 1853.* San Francisco, 1853.
California Senate. *Governor's Special Message, January 30, 1852.* San Francisco, 1852.
De Bow, J. D. B. *Statistical View of the United States . . . Being a Compendium of the Seventh Census.* Washington, D.C.: Government Printing Office, 1854.
Los Angeles County Board of Education. *Annual Report, 1883–1884.* Los Angeles: Morley and Freeman Book Job Printers, 1888.
McPherson, William, ed. *Revised Ordinances of the City of Los Angeles.* Los Angeles: Office of the Los Angeles Star, 1869.
United Nations, Population Division. *The Determinates and Consequences of Population Trends.* New York: United Nations Printing Office, 1953.

U.S. Department of Commerce, Bureau of the Census. *Current Population Reports, November 1969*. Washington, D.C.: Government Printing Office, 1969.

————. *The United States Census, 1960*. Washington, D.C.: Government Printing Office, 1963.

————, Social and Economic Statistics Administration. *General Social and Economic Statistics, California*, pp. 6–751. Washington, D.C.: Government Printing Office, April 1972.

————. *Fifteenth Census of the United States*, "Population." 1 Washington, D.C.: Government Printing Office, 1931.

————. *Compendium of the Tenth Census (June 1, 1880)*. Washington, D.C.: Government Printing Office, 1883.

————. *The Statistics of the Population of the United States in 1870*. Washington, D.C.: Government Printing Office, 1872.

————. *Population of the United States in 1860*. Washington, D.C.: Government Printing Office, 1864.

————. *Statistics of the Population of the United States . . . Being a Compendium of the Seventh Census*. Washington, D.C.: Government Printing Office, 1854.

————. *U.S. Census of Population, 1850*. Washington, D.C.: Government Printing Office, 1852.

U.S. Department of State. *The United States vs. Mexico in the Matter of the Case of the Pious Fund of the Californias*. Washington, D.C.: Government Printing Office, 1903.

Index

"A Mi María Antonia", 72
Acuña, Rodolfo, 31, 103
La Adoración de los Animos en
  Purgatorio, 168
Aguilar, Cristobal, 88, 109
Alemany, Right Reverend
  Joseph Sadoc, 161
Alanis, Felipe, 7
Allport, Gordon, 127
Alvarado rebellion, 8, 19, 20
Amador, José, María, 10–11
Amat, Right Reverend Taddeus,
  161, 164, 167
Los Amigos del Pais, 137–138.
Anglo-Americans: early settlers
  of Los Angeles, 22; and
  Californio newspapers, 152;
  in Mexican-American
  organizations, 151–153
Argüello, Santiago, 24
Aries, Phillippe, 96
Arnaz, José, 65
Associations, growth of,
  134–138
Ávila, Enrique, 28
Ávila, José María, 21

Bancroft, Hubert Howe: rancho
  life, 13–14; on land grants, 30;
  as a source for Mexican-
  American family history,
  77–78 n
Bandidni, Juan, 22
Banditry: as social rebellion,
  109; Juan Flores, 109–110;
  Tiburcio Vasquez, 113–115;
  Joaquin Murieta, 113–114
Baptisms, 1844–1873, 79
Barrio: origin of name, 139; in
  Santa Fe, 139–140. See also
  Sonora Town

Barton, sheriff killed by Flores,
  110
Berryesa, Frémont accused of
  murdering, 157
Bidwell, John, 22
Birthrate: for
  Mexican-Americans, 34, 80;
  decline of, 79, 83
Blauner, Robert, 103
Botello, Narciso, 168
Buchanan, James, in 1856
  election, 157
Bustamente, Francisco, 85

Los Caballeros de Trabajo, 135
California State Constitutional
  Convention, 153–154
Californios: cultural
  distinctiveness, 10–13;
  politics, 19–21, 24–25; in
  Mexican War, 26–27; class
  system, 11–12, 14, 31;
  economic decline, 42–46;
  weddings, 63–64
Calle de los Negros, 141
Calpulli. See Barrio
Cardona, S. A., editor of La
  Crónica, 128
Carillo, José Antonio, 27, 138,
  153, 154
Castro, José de, 24, 27
Catholic Church: priests in Los
  Angeles, 61; construction,
  169–170. See also Plaza
  Church
Cattle, decline of industry in
  Southern California, 42
Cantua Canyon, 114
Celis, Elegio de, 28, 135
Celis, Pastor de, 128
Census: Mexican era, 7;

Census: *(cont.)*
  under-enumeration, 34 n;
  1852 state census, 40,
  179–180; as evidence of
  segregation, 144–145
Chapman, Alfred B., 46
Chavez, Julian, 164
"Chingichnich", creator god, 3
Cholos, 11, 25
"Chukit", virgin god, 3
"Chungichnich". *See*
  "Chingichnich"
Cinco de Mayo, 131, 135
City directories, accuracy of,
  188–190
City Guard, 109, 135
El Clamor Público, 72, 88, 109,
  121, 152
El Club Dramático Español, 73
El Club Musical
  Hispano-Americano, 135
Collins, Randall, 104
Common Council: education,
  89; Sunday laws, 131;
  bilingual schools, 138
Community property, 69. *See
  also* Marriage
"Compadrazgo", duties of
  godparents, 97–98
Compañía Militar, 134
Coronel, Antonio F.: on
  women, 73; school board,
  88–89; chairman of
  Democratic Committee, 154;
  candidate for mayor, 157,
  158; mentioned, 109, 164
Coronel, Ygnacio, 7, 24, 85, 88,
  98
Corte Colón, 151
Coser, Lewis, theory of internal
  conflict, 19–20
Cota, Antonio, 28
Cota, Leonardo, 26
Court system,
  misrepresentation, 116
Covarrubias, Juan M., 154
Crime, Mexican-Americans
  sentenced for, 117–119, and n
La Crónica: on Vasquez'
  banditry, 114; protest
  conditions in barrio, 128, 131;
  Anglo participation in, 152;
  on fiestas, 167–168
Curanderos, 3, 168

Death rate, 66
Democratic party:
  Mexican-American
  participation in, 154–155; bolt
  from, 155–156
Discrimination, in legal system,
  116–119. *See also* Court
  system; Segregation
La Doctrina Católica, 87
Dominguez, Manuel, 154, 158
Las Dos Repúblicas: on
  lynchings, 107–108; on
  Mexican Independence
  celebrations, 132; on religion,
  169; on suicide, 171
Downey, John G., 45

El Eco de la Patria, 119, 122
Education: in the Mexican era,
  84–85; first schools, 85, 88,
  89; school attendance, 85, 87;
  attitudes towards, 87–88;
  bilingual schools, 88–89, 138;
  literacy, 90–92, 90 n
La Escuela Católica, 88
La Escuela de la Concepción
  Imaculada, 89
La Estrella, 120
Ethnic group emergence,
  theories of, 103–105

Family: types of, 67 n, 97, 98;
  size of, 83, 83 n;
  methodology, 183–184
Fárias, Gomez, 6
Fertility, 79, 92. *See also*
  Birthrate
Fiestas, 18, 167
Flores, Juan, as social bandit,
  109–110
Flores, María, 26
Folk medicine. See *Curanderos*
Foster, Stephen C., 29, 153
Fraternal Order of La Corte
  Colón. *See* Corte Colón
Frémont, Captain John C.: as
  military governor, 27–28;
  candidate for president, 155,
  156, 157

Galvez, José, visitador, 4
García, Mario, 32
Gárfias, Manuel, 27
Gente de razón, defined, 12

Geographic mobility, 38,
    149–150, 190
George, Henry, 30
Gerrymandering, 146, 151
Gillespie, Captain Archibald, 26
Godparents. *See*
    "Compadrazgo"
"The Greaser Law", 115
Guardía Zaragosa, 135
Guerra, María Teresa de la, 64
Guerra, Pablo de la, 116, 154
Guerrero, Vicente, 29
Gwin Land Act, 30, 42

de Haro, Frémont accused of
    murdering, 157
Hartnell, William E. P., 64
Hastings, Lansford, 23
Hayes, Judge Benjamin, 41–42,
    107
Híjar, José María, 6
Hobsbawm, Eric, 109–110
Hughes, Charles, 32

Indians of Los Angeles: culture,
    1–4, 5; assimilation of, 13–14
Infant mortality, 80
Immigration: Mexican, 6,
    34–35, 38–41; Anglo-
    American, 22–23. *See also*
    Repatriation
El Instituto Patríotico, 88
La Integridad, 124
Internal colonialism, 103
Irving, Captain John (Red), 107
Islas, Jesús, 121–122

Jenkins, Deputy Constable
    William, 108
Jones, Commodore Thomas
    Catesby, 24
El Joven, 128
Júarez, Benito, 132
La Junta Defensora de la
    Seguridad Pública, 21
La Junta Para Promover la
    Emigración de Todos los
    Hispanos-Americanos
    Residentes en California,
    122–123
La Junta Patriótica de Juárez,
    135
La Junta Patriótica Mexicana,
    151

Juries, Mexican-American
    representation, 117

Kearney, General Stephen, 27
Know-Nothing Party, 115
Kwan, Kian, 104

Land grants, 5
Laslett, Barbara, 183–184
Lawyers, Mexican-American,
    116–117
Lestrade, Reverend Anciluctus,
    161,169
Lincoln, Dr., ferryman at Yuma
    crossing, 38
Lopez y Rivas, Gilberto, 103
Los Angeles: first settlement,
    5–7; government in Mexican
    era, 21; Mexican War in,
    25–26; population growth of,
    6, 7–9, 9 n, 32–34
Los Angeles Express, 114
Los Angeles Star. See La Estrella
Los Lanceros, 134
Lugo affair, 106–107
Lugo, Chico, 106
Lugo, José Carmen del, 14, 153
Lugo, José María, 106
Lugo, Menito, 106
Lynchings, 106, 107, 110, 115

McCleland, Robert Glass, 30
McWilliams, Carey, 75
Manifest Destiny, 157
Marriage: legislation affecting,
    68–69; common law, 67–69;
    Mexican customs, 64–65;
    working women, 67;
    intermarriage, 75–77; and
    romantic love, 70–73; wives'
    age, 77
Martinore, A., speculator, 153
Mason, Colonel Richard B., 153
Mexican Constitution of 1824,
    20–21
Mexican Independence Day,
    73–74, 131, 151–152
La Mexicanita, school, 88
Mexican War in Los Angeles,
    25–29
Micheltorena revolt, 1845, 8, 19
Missions, mentioned, 6, 12, 110,
    121
Molla, Señora Laura, 73

El Monte Boys, 109, 110
Monteverde, Florencio, 121
Moore, Joan, 103
Mora, Right Reverend
    Francisco, 161
Moreno, Right Reverend
    Francisco Diego y, 161
"La Mujer", 72
Murder rate in Los Angeles,
    105–106
Murieta, Joaquin, 113–114. See
    also Banditry
Mutualistas, 136–138

Neve, Governor Felipe de, 5
Newmark, Harris, 18, 110, 116
Newspapers, Spanish language,
    125–126, 127
New Urban History, 177
Nielson, Jose R., 88
"Nigger Alley". See Calle de los
    Negros
Nuestra Señora La Reina de Los
    Angeles, church, 79

Occupations: structure of,
    52–53, 54, 60; classification of,
    185–186; skilled crafts, 57–58
Olvera, Augustín, 27, 109, 116,
    164
Ord, Angustias de la Guerra, 27

Padrés Híjar expedition, 6–7
Padrés, José María, 6
Palomares, Ignacio, 29
Parsons, Talcott, 92
Persistence rate, 35–38. See also
    Geographic mobility ·
Pico, Andrés, 27, 109, 113, 121
Pico, Jesús, 27
Pico, Pío, 21, 24–25, 27, 28
Pico, Solomon, 107
Pico House, 128
Pierce, Franklin, election of
    1856, 157
Pious Fund, 164
Pitt, Leonard, 30, 75
El Plan de Los Angeles, 26
Plaza Church. See Nuestra
    Señora La Reina de Los
    Angeles
Plaza homes, 17
Plenary Council of Bishops, 164

Politics, Californio decline
    analyzed, 158–159, 160
Population estimates, 38, 39 n,
    118 n
Portolá, Captain Gaspar de, 4
Prejudice: theories of, 104–105,
    127; and legal system,
    115–117. See also Segregation
Property holders, 46, 47; and
    persistence, 47–51; and family
    size, 84 and n
Prostitution, 70
Public works, 33

Raho, Father Bernardo, 161
Ramirez, Francisco P.: on
    education, 88; on lynching,
    109; on banditry, 113; on
    prejudice, 115–116, 127; on
    repatriation, 122; on
    American patriotism, 152;
    endorses Republican party,
    157
Ramirez, José, 116
Ranchos: idylic image of, 13, 14;
    rodeos, 17; mentioned, 18, 27,
    41, 45, 106. See also
    Californios
La Raza, development of
    concept, 133–134
"La Raza Cósmica", 133
Record linking, 36–37 n
Reglamento, of 1779, 5
Reid, Hugo, 22, 153
Religion, folk practices,
    167–168
Repatriation, 120, 123–124
Requena, Manuel, 23, 164
Rico, Francisco, 27
El Río de Nuestra Señora La
    Reina de Los Angeles de
    Porciúncula, 4, 5
Rivas, Jesús, 106, 107
Robidoux, Louis, 116
Rodriguez, Francisco, 168
Rodriguez, José, 128
Romero, Josefa, 168
Rubio, Father Gonzales, 161
Ruiz affair, 108–109
Ruiz, Antonio, 108

St. Vincents' College, 89
Salazar, José, 28

Sanchez, Tomás, 109, 113
Sanchez, Vicente, 17
Sandoval, Cipriano, 107
San Juan Day, 168. *See also*
    Fiestas
San Pascual, battle of, 27
Sansevain, Juan, 164
Savaleta, Doroteo, 107
Segregation, 141–143, 147–148,
    146 and n. *See also* Prejudice;
    Sonora Town
Sennett, Richard, 96
Sepúlveda, Antonio, 160
Sepúlveda, Francisco, 17
Sepúlveda, José, 29, 164
Sepúlveda, Juan, 153
Sepúlveda, Ygnacio, 10, 116,
    152–153, 159–160
Serenade, 40–71
La Serenade, 71
Serra, Fray Junípero, 4
Sex ratio, 80. *See also* Birthrate
Shibutani, Tamotsu, 104
Shoshonean. *See* Indians of Los
    Angeles
Sisters of Charity, 164
Skilled workers, 57–58
Small pox, 131
Social banditry. *See* Banditry
La Sociedad de Colonización de
    Nativos de California para el
    Estado de Sonora, 120
La Sociedad
    Hispano-Americana, 151
La Sociedad
    Hispano-Americana de
    Beneficia Mutua, 136–137,
    138
Socioeconomic mobility, 54, 89
    and n, 92, 96, 99
Sonora Town: social conditions,
    128–129, 149–150; changing
    boundaries of, 147–149;
    significance of, 140, 150;
    mentioned, 40, 70, 140, 141
Spanish American Republican
    Club, 134

Spanish language, slang, 124
Stearns, Abel, 22, 29, 153, 164
Stockton, Commodore Robert
    F., 1, 25
Suicide, 171
Sunday laws, 115, 131. *See also*
    Prejudice

El Teatro Alcaron, 73
Temple, John, 22
Teodoli, E. F., 138
de Toro, Juan, 131, 132–133
Torres, Francisco, 107
Treaty of Guadalupe Hidalgo,
    28, 30, 42, 62, 108

U. S. District Court, 119 n

del Valle, Reginaldo, 89, 135
del Valle, Ygnacio, 17, 24,
    69–70, 164
Vallejo, Mariano, 154
Varela, Mariano J., 128
Varela revolt, 25, 26, 109
Varela, Serbulo, 25, 26
Vasconcelos, José, 133
Vasquez, Tiburcio, 109,
    113–115. *See also* Banditry
Verdaguer, Father Peter, 161
Verdugo, Julio, 45
Vignes, Louis, 22, 88

Warner, Juan José, 22, 153
Weber, David J., 104
Wilson, "Don Benito", 22, 24
Wolfskill, William, 22
Women: working, 14, 73;
    education of, 72; heads of
    families, 65–67. *See also*
    Marriage
Workman, William, 24, 151
Wrigley, Edward A., 79–80

Yang-na Indians, 5, 70, 140. *See
    also* Indians of Los Angeles

Zavaleta, Doroteo, 106

Printed in the United States
3877

9 006

9 780520 047730